A High School Plan for Students with College-Bound Dreams

Workbook

This workbook belongs to:

_____

Graduating class of:

_____

A High School Plan for Students with College-Bound Dreams
Workbook

M Y C H A L   W Y N N

Other books by the author:

A High School Plan for Students with College-Bound Dreams
A Middle School Plan for Students with College-Bound Dreams
A High School Plan for Bermudian Students with College-Bound Dreams
A Middle School Plan for Bermudian Students with College-Bound Dreams
College Planning for High School Students: A Quick Guide
College Planning for Middle School Students: A Quick Guide
Don't Quit
Follow Your Dreams: Lessons That I Learned in School
The Eagles who Thought They were Chickens

A High School Plan for Students with College-Bound Dreams: Workbook

Second Edition, 2008
Printing   1

ISBN-13: 978-1-880463-80-2
ISBN-10: 1-880463-80-6
Copyright © 2006 Mychal Wynn
Copyright © 2006 Rising Sun Publishing, Inc.

Credits:
Cover design by Mychal Wynn.
Student Photographs taken by Mychal Wynn.
Illustrations by Mychal-David Wynn.

RISING SUN
PUBLISHING

P.O. Box 70906
Marietta, GA 30007-0906
770.518.0369/800.524.2813
FAX 770.587.0862
E-mail: info@rspublishing.com
Web site: http://www.rspublishing.com

Printed in the United States of America.

Acknowledgments

I would like to acknowledge my wife, Nina, who, as a wife, mother, confidant, and business partner has greatly contributed to the ideas contained within this book. She has put into practice the strategies as she has successfully guided our older son's oftentimes complex and frequently frustrating journey from preschool through high school, into Amherst College. She has also inspired, enlightened, and encouraged other children and their families along their parallel journeys from preschool into college.

I would also like to thank my nieces, Tishandra de Courcy and Kymberly McKay, for their efforts in ensuring that this workbook is usable and doable for any student in any situation.

Lastly, I would like to thank my mother and father who encouraged, sacrificed, and inspired me to become the first college graduate in our family.

Dedication

This book is dedicated to my sons, Mychal-David and Jalani, the thousands of students and parents I meet each year who have college-bound hopes and aspirations, and to those who sacrifice each day on behalf of students and their dreams.

Table of Contents

Introduction

This workbook provides activities and strategies taken from the book, *A High School Plan for Students with College-Bound Dreams*. You should refer to the book for a more comprehensive set of strategies, data, and reference sources. We followed the strategies to help our older son develop his passion for art. A passion that was continually nurtured in his journey from elementary school, through middle school and into high school. Ultimately, he narrowed his list of colleges to the Savannah College of Art and Design, the Ivy League school of Dartmouth, and the top liberal arts college, Amherst College. Following the steps outlined in the book, he applied to and was accepted, via Early Decision, into Amherst College. While our younger son has different passions, he is utilizing similar strategies and well into his college planning as he enters high school.

Whatever your passions—talking, writing, drawing, composing or performing music, entrepreneurship, science, mathematics, politics, athletics, or teaching—there is a college where you can explore your passions and a college setting where you can continue your growth and development into adulthood.

The opportunity to attend college is one that every young person deserves, yet one that far too many deny themselves by squandering their high school years. Whatever your financial situation and whatever your passions, preparing a quality application package and preparing for the rigors of college-level work will provide you with many college opportunities.

Whatever your passions you must develop a plan. Follow the steps and apply the strategies contained within this workbook to develop your plan. Boxes will refer you to page numbers in the *book* for further reading on issues relating to the college planning and college admissions process. Refer to and update the worksheets throughout your four years of high school and refer to them during each meeting with your counselor, and discussions with your parents, as you plan your course schedule, schedule your standardized tests (i.e., SAT and ACT), and identify the summer programs and extracurricular activities that you will participate in.

Have You Prepared for Academic Success?

❑ *I am organized:* I have binders for each subject, with tabs, the course syllabus, teacher e-mail or web site, and grading policy.

❑ *I have before- and after-school routines:* Based on my class schedule and extracurricular activities, I have established routines to ensure that I study, complete my homework, and am well prepared for tests and quizzes.

❑ *I have developed consistent classroom routines:* I have developed classroom routines, which ensure that I make note of homework assignments and test dates, and keep my subject-area binders organized.

❑ *I know how to take good notes:* I have developed effective note-taking skills.

❑ *I engage in a daily review of my notes:* I have established a time within my daily routine to review my notes from each class.

❑ *I engage in a daily review of my agenda:* I have established a time to review my agenda to ensure that I am aware of announced tests, quizzes, and project due dates.

❑ *I engage in effective test preparation:* I have developed the necessary routines to ensure that I am prepared for announced tests and quizzes.

❑ *I have an effective method of filing my homework and graded assignments:* I have developed a routine to ensure that I file graded assignments and that I do not misplace homework.

❑ *I am consciously developing my vocabulary, writing, and grammar skills:* I am consciously expanding my vocabulary and developing my writing and grammatical skills so that I may effectively communicate my thoughts and ideas, and perform well on the SAT and ACT exams.

❑ *I am a critical thinker:* I use critical-thinking skills in my daily decision-making. I consciously go through the process of investigation, interpretation, and judgment when formulating ideas and making decisions.

[Taken from, "A Middle School Plan for Students with College-Bound Dreams"]

Who this book is for

As a fourth-grader, Jalani Wynn, was already focused on college and well into his college plan.

This workbook has been written for students with college-bound dreams and supports the book, *A High School Plan for Students with College-Bound Dreams*. While thousands of students affirm college-bound dreams, far too many are not aware of the importance of using their four years of high school to prepare themselves for college, make themselves a competitive candidate in the admissions process, or do what is necessary to acquire enough financial aid to pay the huge cost of college tuition, room, and board.

Within this group of students are highly-motivated young people who are enrolled in all honors and AP classes and yet have no extracurricular activities or community service to supplement their stellar academic credentials; students who are involved in sports and extracurricular activities, but who are taking the easiest possible academic schedule (and still putting forth only enough effort to be 'C' students); and students who are saying they plan to go to college, but who do not have any idea as to what is needed, how much work is involved, or how to prepare themselves to succeed should they successfully navigate the many hurdles of meeting their high school graduation requirements and admission criteria into a major college or university.

No matter which group of students you fall into, where you want to go to college, where your parent(s) want you to go to college, or where your counselors, coaches, aunts, uncles, mentors, or best friends are encouraging you to go to college, this workbook has been written to assist you and those who are supporting and encouraging you in the pursuit of your college-bound dreams.

Test your current college knowledge by taking the *College Literacy Quiz* on the following pages.

College Literacy Quiz

1. What are AP and IB courses?

   _____

   _____

   _____

2. When are AP exams given and what scores typically qualify for college credit?

   _____

   _____

   _____

3. Who administers the AP and IB Programs?

   _____

   _____

   _____

4. What does the 'weight,' of such courses mean?

   _____

   _____

   _____

5. Is the Ivy League an athletic or academic grouping of colleges?

   _____

   _____

   _____

6. How many colleges make up the Ivy League?

_____

7. What does HBCU stand for?

_____

8. How many HBCUs are there?

_____

9. What is the difference between the SAT I, SAT II, and the ACT and what is the top score for each exam?

_____

_____

_____

10. How many times can you take the SAT I and ACT?

_____

11. Which type of high school classes will best prepare you for success on the Critical Reading and Writing Sections of the SAT I?

_____

_____

_____

12. What advantage, if any, is there to taking the SAT I or ACT more than once?

_____

_____

_____

_____

13. What does PSAT stand for and in which grade (i.e., 9th, 10th, 11th, or 12th) do the scores qualify students as National Merit or National Achievement Scholars?

_____

_____

_____

14. What does GPA mean?

_____

15. What is a weighted GPA?

_____

_____

_____

16. With what organization does a college-bound athlete have to register?

_____

17. What is the significance of taking classes for high school credit while in middle school?

_____

_____

_____

18. What is joint or dual enrollment?

_____

_____

_____

_____

19. What is the significance of taking advanced math classes in middle school?

_____

_____

_____

20. What is the most important academic skill that colleges want incoming students to demonstrate?

_____

_____

_____

21. Does a student from a top private school have a significantly better chance of being admitted to college over a student from an average public high school?

_____

22. What are complimentary sports and how can they increase your college admissions opportunities?

_____

_____

_____

23. Will being a top academic achiever and having high SAT I/ACT scores guarantee that you will be accepted into the college of your choice?

_____

24. Will average grades and average SAT I/ACT scores guarantee that you will not be accepted into the college of your choice?

_____

25. Who is a legacy student?

_____

_____

26. What is FAFSA, why is it important, and when should you complete it?

_____

_____

_____

27. What is EFC?

_____

28. What is Need-based–Need-blind admissions?

_____

_____

_____

29. What is an articulation agreement?

_____

_____

_____

30. How many colleges can a student apply to under the Early Decision program?

_____

_____

_____

(see page 98 for answers)

Why should I care?

After reviewing the college literacy quiz you may be one of those students who is highly literate when it comes to understanding the college admissions process. On the other hand, you may be one of those students who found yourself saying, "Why should I care? I am the best point guard in the city. I am going to get a basketball scholarship." Or, you may be a student who thinks, "Why should I care about AP or IB classes? I am going to take the easiest possible course load and get straight A's. All a college really cares about are the grades that I receive, not the classes that I take."

Whatever you think you know about the college admissions process, you must understand your high school graduation requirements.

1. What are the course requirements for admission into the state universities in your state?

Math: # of years _____ highest level required _____

Science: # of years _____ highest level required _____

# of lab sciences _____ what are the lab sciences at your school?

_____

_____

Social sciences: # of years _____ Foreign language: # of years _____

English: # of years _____

2. Are high school exit or graduation exams given in your school district? If so, what are they?

_____

_____

_____

3. Is there an advantage to declaring a college major? If you answer 'Yes,' explain.

_____

_____

_____

4. What is a 'High School Profile' and why do colleges request them?

_____

_____

5. What is the significance of 'Class Rank' in your state university system? What about private or competitive colleges?

_____

_____

6. How many, and what type of diplomas can you receive from your high school?

_____

_____

_____

7. Can an athlete graduate from high school and still be ineligible to compete in college? If you answer 'Yes,' explain.

_____

8. Can an athlete with a 4.0 GPA still be declared ineligible by the NCAA Clearinghouse? _____

9. Can a student with a 4.0 GPA still be denied admission into a state university? _____

10. Can a student with average grades and average SAT or ACT scores, be admitted into a highly competitive college? _____

(see page 101 for answers)

What you have to do

All of the information contained within this book, resources and web sites to which you will be referred, and ideas and strategies are directed toward the singular mission of preparing you to attend and graduate from college. As a high school student you do not have to have a perfect plan. You do not have to know what you want to study, what career you want to pursue, or even what you aspire to do after graduating from college. You do, however, need a general sense of the type of college experience you want and the amount of effort you are willing to devote to your plan.

Begin with the end in mind

What are your dreams and aspirations—the places you want to go, things you want to experience, changes you want to make in your home, community, or in the world itself? Where do you find your joy? What type of people do you prefer being around? What type of job would you do even if you did not get paid to do it? Or, better yet, what is your purpose? Are you passionate about music, art, science, math, sports, or social issues? Do you prefer working with people or in isolation? Do you have a passion  to coach on the field or run front-office operations? Do you have a passion to teach elementary school children or inspire college students? Would you prefer to write a book, give a lecture, or both? Answering such questions as you enter high school will help you to identify the classes that will expand your knowledge, nurture your passions, and best prepare you for the college experience you are interested in pursuing.

Answering such questions will also greatly enhance your college search as you begin looking for and focusing on colleges that will provide you with the opportunity to pursue your dreams and aspirations. While many students think in terms of attending their "dream college," you will be on your way to attending the "college that will help you to pursue your dreams."

Follow Your Dreams

In the book, *Follow Your Dreams: Lessons That I Learned in School,* I share my experiences growing up in poverty and the academic, social, and emotional struggles I experienced from elementary through high school. While I entered college in the pursuit of a career (electrical engineering), my college education enabled me to discover and to pursue my second-grade passion— writing and talking! If I had known that my elementary school passions could have become my career, I would have chosen different high school classes, a different college major, and explored a much broader range of colleges and universities (I only considered and applied to one college— Northeastern University).

Your dreams, and the colleges that may best help you to pursue those dreams, should guide your efforts in planning your high school schedule of classes, extracurricular activities, and involvement in student and community organizations.

List 5 obstacles that you will have to overcome:

1. _____

2. _____

3. _____

4. _____

5. _____

List 5 academic strengths:

1. _____

2. _____

3. _____

4. _____

5. _____

List 5 academic weaknesses:

1. _____
2. _____
3. _____
4. _____
5. _____

List 5 people who support you:

1. _____
2. _____
3. _____
4. _____
5. _____

List 5 high school goals:

1. _____
2. _____
3. _____
4. _____
5. _____

List 5 life goals:

1. _____
2. _____
3. _____
4. _____
5. _____

The high school through college journey will be an 8-year experience for most students—four years of high school and four years of college. Although it may appear to be a long time away as you enter into the ninth grade, the years will quickly pass and there will be a variety of opportunities to learn, grow, and discover yourself. Take a moment to reflect on what you like to do today and it may help you to better understand the type of people and opportunities you would like to experience over the course of the next four years of high school and what you may want to eventually study in college.

List the things you most enjoy doing:

_____

_____

_____

_____

_____

_____

_____

_____

_____

_____

_____

_____

List the type of people and places you enjoy:

_____

_____

_____

_____

_____

_____

_____

_____

_____

_____

_____

_____

_____

_____

_____

_____

List the types of careers that will allow you to do those things on your first list and work with the type of people or live in the places on your second list:

_____

_____

_____

_____

_____

_____

_____

_____

_____

_____

_____

_____

_____

_____

What type of job would you do even if you did not get paid to do it?

_____

_____

_____

_____

_____

_____

_____

_____

_____

_____

_____

_____

_____

_____

_____

_____

_____

What classes, programs, or camps are you interested in participating?

_____

_____

_____

_____

_____

_____

_____

_____

_____

_____

_____

_____

_____

_____

_____

_____

What are you planning to do after high school?

_____

_____

_____

_____

_____

_____

_____

_____

_____

_____

_____

_____

_____

_____

4-YEAR COLLEGE
COMMUNITY COLLEGE
TRADE SCHOOL
TRAVEL
JOB CORPS
PEACE CORPS
START BUSINESS
MISSIONARY
JOB
PROFESSIONAL SPORTS
ARM FORCES

How would you respond to the question, "What is your purpose?"

_____

_____

_____

_____

_____

_____

_____

_____

_____

_____

_____

_____

_____

_____

_____

_____

Make a collage

Create a collage, poster, or portfolio of images (news articles, magazines, book covers, or original drawings) that reflect your dreams and passions. As you progress through high school you are likely to establish many types of goals, e.g., athletic, academic, social, and creative. Some goals will be easily accomplished while others will require more time and effort. Visualizing your dreams, setting goals, developing your plan, and maintaining your focus over the coming high school and college years can turn today's dreams into tomorrow's reality.

Your Life List

The book, *Chicken Soup for the Soul*, shares the story of a young boy, who, at fifteen years old sat down at his kitchen table in Los Angeles, California, and wrote three words at the top of a yellow pad: 'My Life List.' On his Life List, John Goddard, an adventurer and explorer, wrote 127 goals. Few people would create such a list; fewer yet would even know the things and places on his list. However, all of us, perhaps not as extensively, can develop our own *Life List*.

Take a moment to reflect on what your life list would be. Use the following questions to guide you:

1. What would you like to explore?

2. What would you like to study?

3. Where would you like to visit?

4. What would you like to accomplish?

A High School Plan for Students with College-Bound Dreams

MYCHAL WYNN

Refer to page 11 for the complete Life List.

After answering such questions and developing your own life list, try to answer the following:

What type of college experience would help you to pursue the things on your list?

1. What would you like to explore?

_____

_____

_____

_____

_____

_____

_____

_____

2. What would you like to study?

_____

_____

_____

_____

_____

_____

_____

3.   Where would you like to visit?

_____

_____

_____

_____

_____

_____

_____

4.   What would you like to accomplish?

_____

_____

_____

_____

_____

_____

_____

Prepare for the work ahead

Preparing for the work ahead requires that you establish a place to store all of your high school information as well as all of the college and financial-aid information you gather over the next four years. There are many things that you will need to do and a good deal of information that you will have to file or organize. Completing the activities will help you to better understand the college planning process. Checking the boxes ❑ as you organize information and perform important tasks will help to ensure that you develop a comprehensive college plan and that you are well prepared for the eventual day that you prepare your college application packages.

❑ Set up a binder and label it "College Planning Notebook."

You are going to use this binder to store such information as grades, test scores, awards, and extracurricular activities experienced throughout high school to which you will refer when applying for scholarships and preparing your college application packages.

❑ Set up the following file folders, tabs, or boxes

- ❑ Academics
- ❑ Activities
- ❑ Personal Qualities
- ❑ Intangibles
- ❑ Financial-Aid
- ❑ Awards
- ❑ College Information
- ❑ Scholarship Information

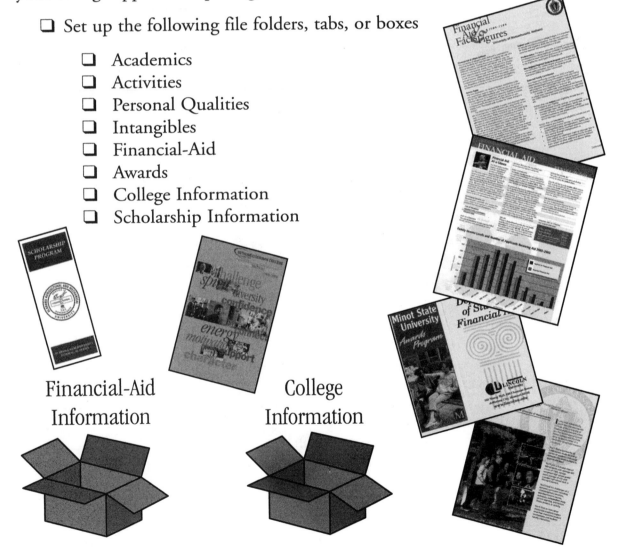

Financial-Aid
Information

College
Information

Working with other students, friends, or family members, develop teams or committees that focus on the areas listed below. You may also use this as an opportunity to create a club to focus on all of the work ahead.

❑ College Admissions

❑ College Fairs

❑ Scholarships

❑ Summer Camps

❑ Internships

❑ Recruited-athletes

❑ College Programs for Juniors and Seniors

❑ Special Interest Programs (e.g., athletics, arts, music, math, science, literary, leadership, etc.)

❑ Local, National, and International Competitions

❑ Tutors

❑ SAT I, SAT II, PSAT, and ACT Prep Programs

❑ Organizing the Application Packages

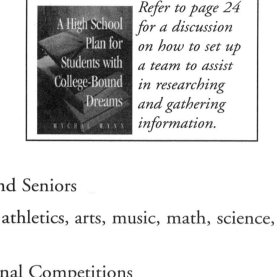

Refer to page 24 for a discussion on how to set up a team to assist in researching and gathering information.

School Information Sheet

Complete this information sheet. You will refer to this information often throughout the college planning process.

H.S. Code (CEEB/ACT): _____ Student ID: _____

Note: If your Student ID is your social security number, you may want to memorize it rather than writing it down here.

School: _____

Address: _____

_____

Phone: _____ FAX: _____

Web site: _____

Principal or Dean: _____

E-mail: _____

Counselor: _____

E-mail: _____

Phone: _____ FAX: _____

Advisor or Career Counselor: _____

E-mail: _____

FAFSA Password: _____PIN: _____DRN: _____

Common Application username: _____Password: _____

Note: You will not receive your FAFSA password and PIN until you begin completing your FAFSA—after January 1 of your senior year.

Parent information (e.g., cell phone, work phone, etc.):

_____

_____

Emergency Contact:

_____

_____

Section I

Academics

Performance in a rigorous curriculum is the single most important aspect of the college application. Colleges want to see a challenging course load through the senior year and an incoming GPA commensurate with their average incoming GPA (3.7, un-weighted at Emory). Emory bases many of its decisions on the history of the high school and on the student's performance in relation to that context.

— [Rock Hard Apps]

Academics

- ❑ Graduation Requirements
- ❑ Test Prep Programs/Resources
- ❑ School Profile/Info
- ❑ Joint/Dual Enrollment, Night School, Summer School, and Online Information
- ❑ Tutors/Tutorial Programs
- ❑ Academic Clubs/Honors
- ❑ Course Catalog
- ❑ Course Schedule
- ❑ Report Cards
- ❑ Test Scores

Why do you want to attend college?

Coming to terms with why you would want to attend college will help you to better understand why your academic focus is important. Have your parent(s) complete this activity and compare your thoughts.

_____

_____

_____

_____

_____

_____

_____

_____

_____

_____

_____

_____

_____

_____

College Affiliations

You can make an important connection to a college through a teacher, counselor, principal, church member, or friend of the family who is a member of the college's alumni association or who has a professional affiliation with the college.

Make note of:

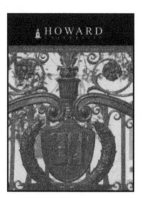

- The college they attended

- Any contacts they may still have at the school

- Any information or insight they may have to assist you in the admissions process

- Any scholarships, grants, or special programs of which they are aware

Name   **College Attended**

_____

_____

_____

_____

_____

_____

_____

_____

Campus Visits, College Tours, and College Fairs

Begin visiting colleges. Take pictures, visit dormitories, talk to students, and get a feel for the type of college community you would like to become a part of. Develop a list of the schools you would like to visit and mark your calendar for college fairs in your area.

Refer to Chapter 1, "Academics," for resources for identifying college fairs and how to prepare for a college fair.

College Research Sheet

Name of College: _____

Highly Competitive • Competitive • Traditional • Open Enrollment

2-yr or 4-yr • Public or Private • In State or Out-of-state

List majors related to your areas of interest:

_____

Credit for AP/IB exams: (Y/N) _____ What scores qualify? _____

SAT IIs required: (Y/N) _____ If so, how many? _____

Average grades/scores of admitted students: GPA _____ ACT _____

SAT: Math _____ Critical Reading _____ Writing _____

Honors Program: (Y/N) _____

Application deadlines:

Early Decision: _____ Early Action: _____ Regular: _____

# of Applicants: _____ Admitted: _____ Application fee: _____

Costs that you would pay as a resident or non-resident:

Tuition: _____ /yr Room/Board: _____ Books: _____

Faculty advisor? (Y/N) _____ Average class size: _____

Diversity (percentage): Asian:_____ Black:_____ Hispanic:_____

White:_____ Native American:_____ Male:_____ Female:_____

To research diversity, go to: www.economicdiversity.org

Graduation rates: 4-yr _____ 6-yr _____

To research graduation rates, go to: www.collegeresults.org

**For comprehensive information on U.S. Colleges and Universities:
www.nces.ed.gov/collegenavigator/**

Pick your top 10 schools

Use your hopes and dreams, and your passions and aspirations to assist you in identifying your top ten schools. As you gather information, talk to people, visit campuses, and account for your financial situation, your list is likely to change as you drop some schools and add new ones.

Refer to page 39 for a listing of the top national universities and liberal arts colleges in the United States.

Get a complete listing of the colleges and universities in your state.

Review or expand your list to ensure that you have identified at least one school in each category (i.e., Highly Competitive, Competitive, and Traditional) in your state of residency. Most states have special scholarship programs and reduced tuition costs for in-state or resident students.

Identify schools within each of the following categories:

❑ *Highly Competitive:* schools with an acceptance rate less than 25 percent.

❑ *Competitive:* schools with an acceptance rate less than 50 percent.

❑ *Traditional:* schools with liberal admissions policies for students meeting their minimum requirements.

❑ *Open Enrollment:* open to anyone who wants to attend.

My Top-Ten List of Colleges and Universities

School	Web site
1.	
2.	
3.	
4.	
5.	
6.	
7.	
8.	
9.	
10.	

High school graduation requirements

High school graduation requirements vary by state—sometimes the requirements vary by district within the state and even by school within the district. It is important for you to identify and understand your state and school district's graduation requirements and track your progress throughout high school.

Refer to Chapter 2, "High School Graduation Requirements" (p. 47) for a complete discussion of high school graduation requirements, meeting NCAA Clearinghouse Guidelines, and preparing for high school exit exams.

State Department of Education Web Site

You may find the necessary information regarding high school graduation requirements, the type of high school diplomas available within your state, and the number and type of high school exit exams on your state department of education web site:

_____

High School Schedule: ❏ **Block** ❏ **8-Period Day** ❏ **Other**

Course	Number of Years	
	Regular	College Prep
History (or Social Sciences)	_____	_____
English	_____	_____
Mathematics	_____	_____
Science/Laboratory Science	_____	_____
Foreign Language	_____	_____
Visual and Performing Arts	_____	_____
College Prep Electives	_____	_____
PE and Health	_____	_____
Other (_____)	_____	_____

What types of diplomas or seals does your high school offer?

Many schools offer general, college prep, and technical diplomas. Some schools also offer special seals (e.g., magnet programs, IB programs, etc.).

List your high school diplomas and seals:

_____

_____

_____

Will you need to pass exit exams to graduate?

At one Georgia high school, upwards of 70 percent of the students had A's and B's on their transcript and yet 90 percent of the students failed the End-of-Grade test in Algebra. In the state of Florida, many students are accepted into college only to be later notified that they failed their high school exit exam, and, therefore, cannot receive their high school diploma.

Exam	Grade the exam will have to be taken

Special requirements for college-bound athletes

If you are planning on participating in college athletics at a Division I or II school during your freshman year in college, you must register with the NCAA Clearinghouse (www.ncaaclearinghouse.net). Many athletes register during the summer between their junior and senior year after receiving their junior-year high school transcript. The Clearinghouse outlines the full range of classes, grades, test scores, and recruiting guidelines as shown in the *NCAA Guide for College-Bound Athletes.*

Download a free copy: www.ncaastudent.org

Before you attend college you have to graduate from high school!

BOSTON, Massachusetts (AP) -- Four attempts. Two points shy.

The numbers plague Karl Kearns, a senior at Burke High School in Boston. This was the first year in which seniors statewide were denied diplomas if they failed the state's high school test, the Massachusetts Comprehensive Assessment System exam, or MCAS.

Kearns was one of some 4,800 seniors who didn't make the cut.

Despite maintaining a "B" average, winning an award for "most improved" in his class, being captain of his football team and overcoming the challenges of a broken home and a reading disability, he didn't score high enough to get a diploma and graduate with his classmates.

[AP Sunday, June 15, 2003]

Diplomas Denied as Seniors Fail Exit Exams

This spring, thousands of high school seniors across the country weren't awarded a high school diploma because they failed to pass their state's exit exam. Lawmakers in states such as California, Florida, Massachusetts, Nevada, and North Carolina have instituted the high-stakes tests to ensure graduates are competent in basic skills, but now they face pressure from angry students and parents to delay or scrap the tests. Students say the tests do not reflect the curriculum covered in school.

"The stuff on the test doesn't equate to anything that I've learned in school," 18-year-old Robyn Collins of Sparks, Nevada protested to the Washington Post. A student with a solid academic record and a 3.0 grade point average, Collins had just failed on her fifth attempt to pass the math portion of the state's exit exam.

[School Reform News, September 1, 2003]

Preparing for high school exit exams in math

Math is a language, and, like becoming proficient in any language, requires daily usage. You should work math problems every day during the school year and at least 3 times a week during the summer months. Continue to review until you can effortlessly speak the language of math, i.e., fractions, binomial, polynomial, quadratic equation, and absolute value.

Test preparation classes

In addition to what you learn in your high school classes, you should take advantage of opportunities for SAT/ACT prep classes and exit exam tutoring. You do not want to sabotage your college opportunities due to low SAT or ACT scores, or worse, failing your high school exit exams!

List SAT/ACT or high school exit exam test preparation classes and the dates you intend to take them:

Where *When*

❑ School _____

❑ Library _____

❑ Boys and Girls Club _____

❑ Private Company _____

❑ _____

❑ _____

Test preparation resources

Test preparation resources, e.g., books, CDs, video tapes, and study guides, may help with both standardized test preparation and some of your current subjects. It is never too soon to begin gathering test preparation materials and referring to them as you continue in your current course work. Reviewing for the SAT/ACT in the 10th and 11th grades will be much better preparation than cramming prior to taking the test.

Make note of test prep resources as you gather them:

❑ College Board (www.collegeboard.com) for SAT prep materials

❑ ACT (www.actstudent.org) for ACT prep materials

❑ _____

❑ _____

❑ _____

Reading, Writing, and Communicating

In the book, *College Admissions Trade Secrets,* Andrew Allen notes:

The dean of admissions for Princeton once said that the best advice he could give to parents is to encourage their children to read. It is that easy and that complex. Most top colleges are more interested in good readers than anything else. A student with an 800-math and a 620-verbal is much more likely to be rejected from a top college than one with an 800-verbal, 620-math.

Refer to Chapter 3, "Course Work" (p. 54) for a complete discussion of the level and type of classes colleges expect students to take.

Increasing your reading and writing skills over the course of your four years of high school will require that you *focus* on increasing your reading and writing skills. Anyone can become a better reader and writer if he or she is willing to apply him or herself.

List the classes, camps, before- or after-school programs that you will use to increase your reading and writing skills:

_____

_____

_____

_____

_____

_____

_____

_____

_____

_____

Honors

You must understand the policy at your high school for taking honors classes and you should plan to enroll into any of the classes you believe you can perform successfully in. Admissions committees will assess a higher value to honors classes.

Refer to page 64 for more about honors classes.

Are additional points awarded for honors classes?   Y/N _____

If you answered yes, indicate the number of additional points: _____

List the honors classes you are interested in taking and speak to your counselor to ensure that you meet any qualifying criteria:

_____

_____

_____

_____

_____

_____

_____

_____

_____

_____

_____

_____

_____

AP (Advanced Placement)

AP classes are college-level classes that are offered to high school students. Some high schools offer a large number of AP classes, others offer only a few classes, and other high schools may not offer any. If your school district offers classes at your high school or at other high schools within the district, you should identify classes you are interested in  *Refer to page 65 for a complete description of the AP program, AP Grade Reports, and AP Scholar recognition levels.*

taking and speak with your counselor about when it would be appropriate to add them to your high school schedule.

Following are some questions you should ask your counselor:

1. What is our school or school district policy for enrollment in AP classes?

   _____

2. Is a teacher recommendation or permission required to enroll in the class?

   _____

3. Are there prerequisite classes, and, if I have not taken the prerequisite classes, can my parents sign a waiver that will allow me to enroll in the class?

   _____

4. Are there mandatory student or parent meetings prior to enrollment?

   _____

5. Is the class limited to certain grades, i.e., junior, senior, etc.?

   _____

6. Will the school district pay the AP exam fee?

   _____

Are additional points awarded for AP classes?   Y/N _____

If you answered yes, indicate the number of additional points: _____

List the AP classes you are interested in taking and speak to your counselor to ensure that you meet any qualifying criteria:

_____

_____

_____

_____

_____

_____

> *You must carefully review each college's AP course exam policy. For example, at Yale, no course credit is awarded for AP Art, AP Political Science, or AP Psychology. 1 credit is awarded for an AP exam score of 4 or 5 in AP Computer Science AB while no credit is awarded for AP Computer Science A. No credit is awarded for AP U.S. History, however, 2 credits are awarded for an exam score of 4 or 5 in AP Art History. One credit is awarded for a 5 on the AP Calculus AB exam while one credit for a 4 and 2 credits for a 5 are awarded on the AP Calculus BC exam.*
>
> *Go to the Yale web site for a listing of qualified classes:*
> *http://www.yale.edu/yalecollege/freshmen/academics/acceleration/table.html*

Review the available AP Scholar awards and list those you are interested in qualifying for:

_____

_____

_____

Review the AP Scholar awards (p. 69) and list those awards you would like to earn.

_____

Joint Enrollment (take college classes while still in high school)

If your high school offers joint or dual enrollment classes you should meet with your counselor to fully understand the enrollment requirements. If you are interested in joint or dual enrollment classes you may use the following checklist to gather your information.

 *Review the Joint Enrollment/ Postsecondary Programs information on page 73.*

College(s) offering joint or dual enrollment programs:

1. _____

2. _____

3. _____

Application deadline: (1) _____ (2) _____ (3) _____

GPA requirement: (1) _____ (2) _____ (3) _____

SAT requirement: (1) _____ (2) _____ (3) _____

ACT requirement: (1) _____ (2) _____ (3) _____

Year you can enroll: (1) _____ (2) _____ (3) _____

Note the joint or dual enrollment classes offered:

1. _____
_____
_____

2. _____
_____
_____

3. _____
_____
_____

GPA Calculation: ❑ 4 Point Scale   ❑ Numeric   ❑ Other

Following is an example for computing GPA on a four point scale. To compute the GPA, add the total number of points (10) (i.e., A=4; B=3; C=2; D=1; F=0) and divide by total classes (4) resulting in a grade point average of 2.5.

GPA Calculation		
Class	Grade	Points
English	A	(4)
Spanish I	C	(2)
Chemistry	D	(1)
Algebra II	B	(3)
Total Points		10

$$\frac{\text{Total Points } 10}{\text{Total Classes } 4} = \text{GPA 2.5 (C+)}$$

Weighted GPA

A weighted GPA reflects a student's actual GPA (un-weighted) plus any additional points awarded for classes such as honors, AP (Advanced Placement), IB (International Baccalaureate), or AT (Academically Talented)—based on your high school's weighted policy. For example, if, the English, Spanish I, and Algebra II classes were honors classes, and your high school awards an additional point for honors classes, the GPA would be higher.

Honors English   **A**
Honors Spanish I   **C**
Chemistry   **D**
Honors Algebra II   **B**

Weighted GPA Calculation		
Class	Grade	Points
Honors English	A	(4+1)
Honors Spanish I	C	(2+1)
Chemistry	D	(1)
Honors Algebra II	B	(3+1)
Total Points		13

$$\frac{\text{Total Points } 13}{\text{Total Classes } 4} = \text{GPA 3.25 (B)}$$

To compute the weighted GPA, add the total number of points (10), plus the additional point for each honors class, and divide by the number of classes (4) resulting in a grade point average of 3.25.

While the un-weighted GPA would be the same (2.5), the weighted GPA would be 3.25.

Numeric Grade Conversion

Since the grading scales vary between school districts (e.g., 90 - 100 = A in one district while 93 - 100 = A in another district) a true GPA conversation requires two steps:

1. Convert the numeric grade to a letter grade for each class based on your school district's grading table (e.g., 70 - 79 = C, 80 - 89 = B; and 90 - 100 = A).

2. After converting the numeric grades follow the conversation tables above to compute the weighted and un-weighted GPA.

Class Rank

Ask your counselor if your school computes class rank and what impact, if any, class rank has on admission into your state university system. For example, Texas has a law that guarantee's resident-students who rank in the top ten percent of their high school graduating class, admission into the student's choice of the state's public universities.

House Bill 588, Sec. 51.803 (1997). AUTOMATIC ADMISSION: ALL INSTITUTIONS.

Each general academic teaching institution shall admit an applicant for admission to the institution as an undergraduate student if the applicant graduated in one of the two school years preceding the academic year for which the applicant is applying for admission from a public or private high school in this state [Texas] accredited by a generally recognized accrediting organization with a grade point average in the top 10 percent of the student's high school graduating class.

Track your GPA for each year of high school

9th Grade: Weighted _____ Un-weighted _____

10th Grade: Weighted _____ Un-weighted _____

11th Grade: Weighted _____ Un-weighted _____

12th Grade: Weighted _____ Un-weighted _____

Track your Class Rank for each year of high school

If your high school tracks your class ranking, make note of it for each year of high school.

9th Grade: _____ 10th Grade: _____

11th Grade: _____ 12th Grade: _____

Compare your academic performance against a college's expectations at the CollegeBoard Academic Tracker web site:
www.collegeboard.com

Set goals

The question for you to ask yourself as you begin the process of developing your high school plan is, "Four years from now, why would a college want to admit me into its freshman class? What will be special about me and what will I be able to contribute to its school community?"

While this workbook may provide you with advice, only you can follow your plan. You must develop the habit of setting goals and making the necessary commitment to pursue your goals.

Begin by writing down each class and setting a goal for the grade you want to earn. Make a copy of this page and do the same for each sport and activity in which you participate.

My Goals

Class or Activity	Goal	Achieved (Y/N)

Entering high school with the passionate desire to pursue something, become something, discover something, change something, or fulfill some purpose will guide your intellectual, spiritual, moral, physical, and creative development in ways, that, four years from now, will enable you to sit in a college interview and say, "I have had a passion to do... since I entered high school; this is what I have done and why I want to continue my studies at your college."

[Taken from, "A High School Plan for Students with College-Bound Dreams," p. 18]

What academic support do you need?

An athlete who wants to get bigger, run faster, or increase his or her skill level identifies a coach, personal trainer, or training partner. There is only so much that we can do by ourselves. We need someone to help us to overcome our weaknesses and maximize our strengths. The same applies to academics. Tutors and support programs provide academic coaching. If you are serious about attending college then you must take overcoming your academic weaknesses and maximizing your academic strengths seriously.

List any areas of academic support you need (e.g., math, science, writing, research, etc.) and the names of tutors or tutorial programs:

_____

_____

_____

_____

_____

_____

_____

As you enter high school, you must openly and honestly assess your strengths and weaknesses. Do you have difficulty with math? Is science one of your weakest areas? Do you struggle with doing research and writing papers? Are you having difficulty grasping a foreign language? Do not allow yourself to get off to a slow start and do not shrug off your weaknesses, "I am just not good at math." You must identify what and whom you need to ensure your academic success throughout high school. Do not make the mistake of believing that a music major will not have to succeed in college math or that an athlete will not have to write a college paper. Even a star athlete, concert pianist, or brilliant artist will need a solid academic foundation to succeed in and graduate from college.

[Taken from, "A High School Plan for Students with College-Bound Dreams," p. 83]

As you prepare to develop your high school plan, keep in mind that no matter what you do, you may simply be blessed with a highly-unusual opportunity. Thousands of students are contacted by or admitted into a particular college, but, not because they are among the highest ranked, have the highest GPA, or have followed the strategies outlined in this book. They are blessed to attract the attention of the college—they play a particular position on an athletic team, they play a musical instrument and the college orchestra is in need of a violinist, they helped a little old lady across the street and her son happened to be a college admissions officer, they received national notoriety as the result of a heroic act, their parent attended the college, their uncle belongs to the same country club as the college's president, their family donated a new athletic facility, or their parents are celebrities. Whatever the reason, you may be one of those students who get *invited* to a particular college or university. "

[Taken from, "A High School Plan for Students with College-Bound Dreams," p. 27]

Important relationships

Developing and executing an effective high school plan will require that you build relationships with several groups of people. Colleges will evaluate your application in part based on recommendations from your teachers and counselor; your meaningful involvement in clubs, organizations, school and community service projects; and your involvement in sports, band, cheerleading, or other special-interest activities. The relationships you develop with tutors and study groups will also greatly contribute to your academic success throughout high school.

List the names of people you can count on to write a positive recommendation. Expand this list as you progress through high school with the names of teachers, counselors, coaches, administrators, and mentors:

_____

_____

_____

_____

_____

_____

Academic clubs

Academic clubs provide a great opportunity for support, encouragement, and enrichment opportunities. If there are no academic clubs at your school, this would be your opportunity to demonstrate leadership skills and start one.

List the academic clubs currently available at your school, organization, or within your community and place a check next to those you will be participating in:

❏ _____

❏ _____

❏ _____

❏ _____

❏ _____

❏ _____

❏ _____

❏ _____

❏ _____

❏ _____

❏ _____

If you are college-bound, then you should try to develop relationships with other college-bound students—students with similar hopes, dreams, and aspirations. If your high school plan includes taking honors and AP classes, then you are going to be in classes with other students who have high aspirations and who are willing to put forth the time and effort to be successful academically. Such individuals may or may not be among your current friends. While some students perform well by reviewing their class notes and studying independently, many students benefit from study groups where they discuss class notes, share ideas, review their work and prepare for tests and exams as a group.

[Taken from, "A High School Plan for Students with College-Bound Dreams," p. 85]

Academic honors

Begin high school with a focus on the types of honors, awards, and recognition you would like to receive. Whether you are interested in qualifying for the honor roll or being recognized in your state's Governor's Honors program, you must set your academic

Refer to Chapter 5, "Academic Honors" (p. 89) for a complete discussion of of academic honors.

goals as you enter high school. Use the worksheet on the following page to make note of your awards as you receive them.

List the academic awards available at your school, organization, or within your community and place a check next to those you will be attempting to qualify for:

❑ _____

❑ _____

❑ _____

❑ _____

❑ _____

❑ _____

❑ _____

❑ _____

❑ _____

❑ _____

❑ _____

❑ _____

❑ _____

❑ _____

❑ _____

Honors/Awards

Description

	9th	10th	11th	12th
_____	___	___	___	___
_____	___	___	___	___
_____	___	___	___	___
_____	___	___	___	___
_____	___	___	___	___
_____	___	___	___	___
_____	___	___	___	___
_____	___	___	___	___
_____	___	___	___	___
_____	___	___	___	___
_____	___	___	___	___
_____	___	___	___	___
_____	___	___	___	___
_____	___	___	___	___
_____	___	___	___	___
_____	___	___	___	___
_____	___	___	___	___
_____	___	___	___	___
_____	___	___	___	___
_____	___	___	___	___
_____	___	___	___	___
_____	___	___	___	___

Plan your schedule

All of the information you need to evaluate classes and plan your high school course schedule is contained within one or more publications available from your high school, school district's offices, or from your state department of education. Course descriptions, GPA calculations, AP course offerings, and exit exam criteria can usually be found through the following resources:

❑ *Student Planner/Agenda*

❑ *School District Curriculum Handbook*

❑ *High School Course Offerings*

Make a copy of these two pages and take them with you to your meeting with your counselor. Ask questions to ensure that you fully understand the prerequisite classes and enrollment criteria. Following are some questions to assist in guiding the discussions with your high school career or guidance counselor:

1. What are the required and recommended courses—for graduation and for college prep?

2. Are there any automatic admissions criteria for state colleges, for example, class rank?

3. Which elective courses do you recommend?

4. I have indicated the honors and AP courses I am interested in taking and I would like to know if there is anything I must do to meet all the prerequisite or enrollment requirements?

5. Can any of my elective or required classes be taken in summer school, night school, or online?

6. Are there tutors or is there a school-sponsored tutorial program that you would recommend?

7. What are your thoughts on the four-year schedule I have developed?

8. When is the PSAT/NMSQT (PSAT National Merit Scholarship Qualifying Test) given?

9. Are there any after school, evening, or special classes available for college planning or SAT/ACT preparation?

10. Do you have college handbooks or other guides that I may browse or borrow? Do you have a copy of the free "Taking the SAT I" booklet that has a practice test in it (www.collegeboard.com)?

11. Do you have a college-planning guide or calendar that outlines the things that I should be doing each year?

12. Is there a list of colleges that have a relationship with, or actively recruit from this school?

13. Are there any college fairs at this school or nearby? If so, how can I find out when they are scheduled?

14. What are the requirements or standards for the honor society?

15. What clubs, organizations, community service, or student activities do you suggest I consider joining or becoming involved in?

16. I have developed my top-ten list of schools. Do you have any information or are there alumni from our school who can provide me with information about any of the schools on my list?

17. Are there any special scholarships or awards I should be aware of so I can begin preparing myself?

18. How does our school compare to others, in terms of test scores, reputation, and ranking?

19. What is the deadline for submitting class requests for the next school year?

Make note of the registration deadline for:

Summer School:

_____

Night School:

_____

Online Programs:

_____

Junior College:

The critical areas to remember are:

- *Take as many honors, AP, or advanced classes as you can*
- *Explore summer school, night school, joint enrollment, and online opportunities*
- *Fully understand prerequisite classes, enrollment criteria, and course sequencing*

Refer to your school district's graduation requirements, diploma guidelines, and the sample schedules on this page to develop a preliminary draft of your four-year high school schedule.

Traditional 8 Period Schedule

High School Schedule of Student Aspiring to be Admitted into Yale, Morehouse, and Amherst College

	Credit
9th	
Honors Accelerated Math I	1
Math Research Methods	1
Honors Biology	1
Honors Freshman Language Arts	1
Honors Spanish II	1
Guitar 1A/1B	1
Intermediate Chorus	1
Political Science/Health & Fitness (online)	1
10th	
Honors Accelerated Math II	1
Honors Chemistry	1
Honors Sophomore Language Arts	1
Honors Spanish III	1
AP Computer Science AB	1
Mixed Chorus	1
Music Theory	1
Honors Economics/World History (online)	1
11th	
Honors Accelerated Math III	1
Honors American Lit/AP Lit and Comp	1
Honors Physics	1
Honors Spanish IV	1
AP U.S. History	1
AP Music Theory	1
Gifted Internship (Performing Arts)	1
12th	
College English	1
AP Calculus BC	1
AP Psychology	1
AP Physics B	1
Advanced Topics in Physics	1
AP Spanish	1
Gifted Internship (Performing Arts)	1

Total Credits Required: 24 • Total Credits Earned: 30

4 x 4 Block Schedule

High School Schedule of Student Accepted into Amherst College
Student College Majors: Fine Arts, Psychology

	Credit
Middle School	
Spanish	1
9th 1st Semester	
Algebra I	1
Spanish II	1
9th Grade Literature	1
Art Fundamentals	1
2nd Semester	
Geometry	1
Spanish III	1
Biology	1
2 Dimensional Design	1
10th 1st Semester	
Honors Algebra II	1
Honors Spanish IV	1
Honors 10th Grade Lit	1
3 Dimensional Design	1
2nd Semester	
AP Computer Science	1
Honors Pre-Calculus	1
Chemistry	1
Drawing/Painting I/II	1
Online Classes	
Honors Economics	.5
Health & Fitness	.5
11th 1st Semester	
AP U.S. History	.5
AP Art Portfolio	1
AP Spanish Language	1
Honors American Lit	.5
Honors Physics	1
2nd Semester	
AP U.S. History (cont.)	.5
Drawing/Painting III/IV	1
Honors Spanish Culture	1
Honors American Lit (cont.)	.5
Honors Bio/Organic Chemistry	1
Online Classes	
World History	1
12th 1st Semester	
AP 2-D Portfolio	1
Jewelry Making	1
World Literature	1
AP Psychology	.5
AP Environmental Science	.5
2nd Semester	
AP 2-D Portfolio (cont.)	1
Political Science	1
Science & Technology	1
AP Psychology (cont.)	.5
AP Env. Science (cont.)	.5

Total Credits Required: 24 • Total Credits Earned: 35

Create sample course schedules based on the type of high school diploma you want to receive and where you intend to apply to college, e.g., highly competitive, competitive, state university, open enrollment, junior or community college, etc. You may want to make copies of these pages and create several course schedules, e.g., very demanding, demanding, average, easy, etc. Use the caption "S" for those classes that will be taken during summer or night school, online, or through joint enrollment.

Course Description	Years	Credit	9th	10th	11th	12th	S

English   (Requirement _____)

————————————————————————   —   —   —   —   —
————————————————————————   —   —   —   —   —
————————————————————————   —   —   —   —   —
————————————————————————   —   —   —   —   —
————————————————————————   —   —   —   —   —

Math   (Requirement _____)

————————————————————————   —   —   —   —   —
————————————————————————   —   —   —   —   —
————————————————————————   —   —   —   —   —
————————————————————————   —   —   —   —   —
————————————————————————   —   —   —   —   —

Science   (Requirement _____)

————————————————————————   —   —   —   —   —
————————————————————————   —   —   —   —   —
————————————————————————   —   —   —   —   —
————————————————————————   —   —   —   —   —
————————————————————————   —   —   —   —   —

Social Sciences   (Requirement _____)

————————————————————————   —   —   —   —   —
————————————————————————   —   —   —   —   —
————————————————————————   —   —   —   —   —
————————————————————————   —   —   —   —   —
————————————————————————   —   —   —   —   —

Course Description	Years	Credit	9th	10th	11th	12th	S

Foreign Lang. (Requirement _____)

_____ — — — — —
_____ — — — — —
_____ — — — — —
_____ — — — — —
_____ — — — — —

Health/PE (Requirement _____)

_____ — — — — —
_____ — — — — —
_____ — — — — —
_____ — — — — —
_____ — — — — —

Arts/Music (Requirement _____)

_____ — — — — —
_____ — — — — —
_____ — — — — —
_____ — — — — —
_____ — — — — —
_____ — — — — —
_____ — — — — —
_____ — — — — —
_____ — — — — —
_____ — — — — —
_____ — — — — —
_____ — — — — —

Other (Requirement _____)

_____ — — — — —
_____ — — — — —
_____ — — — — —
_____ — — — — —
_____ — — — — —

Total Credits Earned _____   Required Credits _____

Total Honors Classes _____   AP Classes _____

Sample High School Transcript (4 x 4 Block Schedule)

Crs ID	Course Title	Grd	Credit	Crs ID	Course Title	Grd	Credit	Crs ID	Course Title	Grd	Credit
North Springs High School				**North Springs High School**				**North Springs High School**			
Grd 09 10/2002 Term: S1				Grd 09 5/2003 Term: S2				Grd 10 3/2004 Term: S2			
Atlanta, GA				Atlanta, GA				Atlanta, GA			
23.0610000				26.4120002				11.0160010			
	9th Lit/Comp	81	0.500		Biology	83	0.500		AP Computer Sci A	80	0.500
27.0610000				27.0630000				27.0670040			
	Algebra I	86	0.500		Geometry	81	0.500		Pre Calculus H	75	0.500
50.4212060				50.4213060				40.4510000			
	Art Fndmntls M	81	0.500		2D Dsgn Block I M	79	0.500		Chemistry	87	0.500
60 0720000				60.0730000				50.4313061			
	Spanish 2	87	0.500		Spanish 3	71	0.500		Draw/Paint 1 M	80	0.500
Crd Att: 2.000 Cmp: 2.000 Numeric Avg: 83.7500				Crd Att: 2.000 Cmp: 2.000 Numeric Avg: 78.5000				Crd Att: 2.000 Cmp: 2.000 Numeric Avg: 84.0000			
North Springs High School				**North Springs High School**				**North Springs High School**			
Grd 09 12/2002 Term: S1				Grd 10 10/2003 Term: S1				Grd 10 5/2004 Term: S2			
Atlanta, GA				Atlanta, GA				Atlanta, GA			
23.0610000				23.0620040				11.0160010			
	9th Lit/Comp	83	0.500		10th Lit/Comp H	84	0.500		AP Computer Sci A	90	0.500
27.0610000				27.0640040				27.0670040			
	Algebra I	76	0.500		Algebra II H	71	0.500		Pre Calculus H	80	0.500
50.4212060				50.4214060				40.4510000			
	Art Fndmntls M	82	0.500		3-D Dsgn Block I M	81	0.500		Chemistry	86	0.500
60.0720000				60.0740040				50.4313062			
	Spanish 2	80	0.500		Spanish 4 H	87	0.500		Draw/Paint 2 M	86	0.500
Crd Att: 2.000 Cmp: 2.000 Numeric Avg: 80.2500				Crd Att: 2.000 Cmp: 2.000 Numeric Avg: 86.0000				Crd Att: 2.000 Cmp: 2.000 Numeric Avg: 89.0000			
North Springs High School				**North Springs High School**				**NGA Summary**			
Grd 09 3/2003 Term: S2				Grd 10 12/2003 Term: S1							
Atlanta, GA				Atlanta, GA				Numeric Avg:	83.7813		
26.4120000				23.0620040					83.7813		
	Biology	88	0.500		10th Lit/Comp H	82	0.500				
27.0630000				27.0640040				HOPE GPA:			
	Geometry	87	0.500		Algebra II H	77	0.500				
50.4213060				50.4214060				Total Credits Attempted:	16.000		
	2D Dsgn Block I M	77	0.500		3-D Dsgn Block I M	83	0.500		Total Credits Earned:	16.000		
60.0730000				60.0740040							
	Spanish 3	75	0.500		Spanish 4 H	85	0.500				
Crd Att: 2.000 Cmp: 2.000 Numeric Avg: 81.7500				Crd Att: 2.000 Cmp: 2.000 Numeric Avg: 87.0000							

Get a profile of your high school

1. Go to www.schoolmatters.com.

2. Find your school and compare to others in your state.

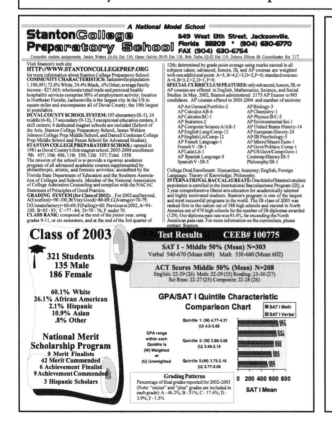

Top colleges will request a copy of your high school's *School Profile*. Some of the information contained in the profile will be average SAT/ACT scores, number and type of advanced classes offered (e.g., honors, AP, etc.), number and description of the type of students attending the school, and how grade point averages are calculated. Subsequently, colleges will know if you took an easy, average, demanding, or very demanding academic schedule.

Track your high school course work, credits earned, and grades

Course Description   **Credits Year**   **Grades**

English (Requirement ____)

Math (Requirement ____)

Science (Requirement ____)

Social Science (Requirement ____)

Course Description

Grades

Credits Year

Foreign Language (Requirement ___)

Health/PE (Requirement ___)

Arts/Music (Requirement ___)

Electives (Requirement ___)

Required Credits ___ Credits Earned ___ Honors Classes ___ AP Classes ___

Un-weighted GPA ___ Weighted GPA ___ Class Rank ___

Academic Camps, Classes, Programs

Use to track classes and participation in academic camps, classes, and programs.

Course/Program Description	Credits	Year	Grades

Standardized Tests

ACT (Top score: 36)

The ACT (American College Testing Exam) is a national college admission examination that consists of tests in English, Mathematics, Reading, Science, and an optional writing section.

ACT results are accepted by virtually all U.S. colleges and universities. The ACT includes 215 multiple-choice questions and takes approximately three hours and 30 minutes to complete with breaks.

Your score is based on the number of correct answers only, so if you are not sure, taking a guess does not hurt.

Go to the following web site to see the type of colleges that your ACT scores qualifies you for admissions:

http://www.actstudent.org/plan/flash/measureup.swf

PSAT (Top score: 80)

The PSAT (Preliminary Scholastic Achievement Test) consists of two 25-minute verbal sections, two 25-minute math sections, and one 30-minute writing skills section.

The PSAT provides practice for the SAT I. As a result of your answers to the PSAT questionnaire, you will begin receiving college information in the mail so be sure to answer the questions carefully and provide an accurate mailing address.

Refer to page 122 for a complete discussion of the SAT, ACT, and PSAT including testing strategies, how the scores compare, and how to register.

Junior-year scores are used to determine qualification for the National Merit and National Achievement Scholar programs.

SAT I (Top score: 2400)

The first SAT I (Scholastic Aptitude Test) was administered in 1926 to 8,040 students. Today more than two million students annually take the SAT I. The most recent change to the SAT I occurred in 2005. The Verbal Section was replaced with the Writing and Critical Reading Sections. The Writing Section consists of a 35-minute multiple choice section and a 25-minute essay. The Critical Reading Section consists of two 25-minute and one 20-minute sections. The Math Section consists of two 25-minute and one 20-minute sections. The SAT I is offered during October, November, December, January, March, May, and June.

Note the testing dates on which you plan to take the SAT I:

9th: _____

10th: _____

11th: _____

12th: _____

The SAT carries a wrong answer penalty (either 1/4 or 1/3 point) with no deduction for blank answers.

Each of the 3 sections (Math, Writing, and Critical Reading) has a top score of 800 points for a total top score of 2400.

SAT II (Top score: 800)

The SAT II consists of tests offered in five Subject areas that are one-hour, mostly multiple-choice tests, designed to measure how much students know about a particular academic subject and how well they can apply that knowledge. Colleges use the test scores primarily for class placement; however, up to three tests may be required for some college admissions. The SAT II is offered during October, November, December, January, May, and June.

List the SAT II subject tests you plan to take:

_____

_____

_____

_____

Note the testing dates on which you plan to take the SAT IIs:

9th: _____

10th: _____

11th: _____

12th: _____

CLEP (College-Level Examination Program)

CLEP is the College-Level Examination Program that provides students with the opportunity to demonstrate college-level achievement through a program of exams in undergraduate college courses. There are 2,900 colleges that grant credit or advanced standing for CLEP exams. Each college publishes its qualifying criteria and number of credits awarded. The qualifying criteria and credits awarded will vary by college.

Talk to your counselor and log on to the College Board web site for more information at *www.collegeboard.org*.

What if I do not test well?

Many colleges place more emphasis on grades, classes taken, extracurricular activities, and what type of student they believe you would be at their school. There is also a growing number of colleges that do not require SAT or ACT scores. Regardless of whether the schools on your top-ten list require SAT or ACT scores or not, keep in mind that your SAT or ACT scores are only one component of your overall college plan.

> *One does not need to score 2400 to gain admission to the most selective schools in America, and that 25 percent of the students admitted to these schools have scores below the ranges some might consider Ivy League–type numbers. Twenty-five percent of Cornell's class of 2003—which in fact is about 800 students—had a best SAT I score below 1270 (on the old SAT). It's safe to say that many more than 800 of the roughly 6500 plus students admitted to Cornell for the class of 2003 also had SAT I scores below 1270 (on the old SAT). Students admitted to highly selective colleges who have scored below mid-range most likely have a major hook—exceptional personal qualities or some other facet that makes them compelling candidates for admission.*

> — *[What It Really Takes to Get into the Ivy League]*

Standardized Tests, AP Exams, Subject Tests

	9th	10th	11th	12th
PSAT				

(Note: 11th-grade PSAT scores are used for National Merit and National Achievement Scholar consideration)

	9th	10th	11th	12th
SAT I				
Critical Reading				
Math				
Writing				
ACT (Overall Composite)				
Reading				
Math				
Science				
Writing				
SAT II				

Average SAT/ACT College Admissions Scores

ACT Composite Score	College Selectivity	SAT I Total Score	Sample Colleges
17 – 20	Open Admissions	1210 – 1410	Bowie State University (MD) City College of New York City College of San Francisco Morgan State University (VA) Norfolk State University (VA)
18 – 21	Liberal Admissions	1290 – 1500	Villa Julie College (MD) Fairmont State College (WV) Bridgewater College (VA) Chowan College (NC)
20 – 23	Traditional	1410 – 1590	Frostburg University (MD) East Carolina University (NC) Hampton University (VA) George Mason University (VA) West Virginia University (WV)
22 – 27	Selective	1530 – 1820	Towson University (MD) Salisbury University (MD) University of Massachusetts Washington College (MD) Clemson University (SC) Spelman College (GA) Florida State University (FL)
27 – 36	Highly Selective	1820 – 2400	Yale University (CT) Amherst College (MA) Juilliard (NY) Cooper Union (NY) Duke University (NC) UNC Chapel Hill (NC) University of Virginia (VA) Georgetown University (DC) Harvard University (MA)

U.S. News and World Report provides a comprehensive
college search and comparison web site:

http://colleges.usnews.rankingsandreviews.com/usnews/edu/college/
rankings/rankindex_brief.php

Section II

Extracurricular

Activities

Along with athletics, music is an extracurricular activity where admissions officers can evaluate an individual's talents and place a value on it in relation to the institutional needs and priorities. Highly selective institutions hold music in high regard, considering it both an academic pursuit and an extracurricular activity. NYU, Yale, and Columbia offer renowned conservatory programs in addition to their strong academic departments. Music departments at other schools offer individualized instruction and opportunities to perform on campus and within the music scene in the area.

— *[What it Really Takes to Get into The Ivy League & Other Highly Selective Colleges]*

Extracurricular Activities

❏ Community Service
❏ Community Programs
❏ Sports
❏ Clubs/Organizations
❏ Competitions
❏ Jobs/Internships
❏ Résumé

Review the clubs, sports, student organizations, and student activities available at your school, organization, or within your community and identify at least two sports, two clubs, two organizations, two activities, and two community service activities or projects to which you are willing to make a four-year commitment:

Community Service:

_____

_____

_____

_____

Community Programs:

_____

_____

_____

_____

Sports:

_____

_____

_____

Clubs & Organizations

21st Century Leaders
4-H
Academic Bowl
American Legion
  Auxiliary Boys
American Legion
  Auxiliary Girls
Aquarium
Art Club
Art Honor Society
Big Brothers/Big Sisters
Biology
Boys & Girls Club
Business Professionals
  of America
Chess
Choir
Church Youth Group
Civil Air Patrol
Color Guard
Computer Club
D.A.R.E.
Debate Team
DECA
Drama
Drill Team
Fellowship of Christian
  Athletes
Friends of the Library
Foreign Language
Future Business
  Leaders of America
FCCLA (Family, Career,
  and Community
  Leaders of America)
Habitat for Humanity
Hugh O'Brian Youth
  Leadership
Junior Achievement
Junior Classical League
Junior Statesmen of
  America
Key

Clubs/Organizations:

_____

_____

_____

_____

Competitions:

_____

_____

_____

_____

Jobs/Internships:

_____

_____

_____

_____

Clubs & Organizations

Letterman
Math Club
Math Honor Society
Model U.N.
Mu Alpha Theta
Music Honor Society
National Beta Club
National FFA
National Forensic
 League
National Honor
 Society
National Young
 Leaders Conference
Outdoors
Pep Squad
People to People Student
 Ambassador Program
Photography
Quill and Scroll Society
Quiz Bowl
R.O.T.C.
Scholastic Bowl
Science Club
Science Honor Society
Scouts: Boy/Girl
Service
Speech Team
Staff Member
 Newspaper
 Yearbook
 Literary Magazine
 Radio Show
 Television Show
Students Against Drunk
 Driving
Student Government
 Advisory Council
 Class Officer
 Student Council
 Class Representative
Technology
Temple Youth Group
Varsity
Vocational Industrial
 Club of America
Young Democrats
Young Republicans

Extracurricular Activities, Work Experience and Volunteer Work

Description	Your Role/Position	Hours Per Wk	Wks Per Yr	9th	10th	11th	12th

Extracurricular Activities, Work Experience and Volunteer Work

Description	Your Role/Position	Hours Per Wk	Wks Per Yr	9th	10th	11th	12th

Keep track of your extracurricular activities

Eventually, you will have to develop a résumé for job interviews, to provide to people who will write recommendation letters for you, to scholarship committees, and to support your college applications.

Tracking what you do, what you learn, and how you benefit from each year's experiences will help you develop your college essays. Use the example on the following page to guide you in developing your résumé.

Sample Résumé

Mychal-David Wynn

P.O. Box 70906
Marietta, GA 30007

Education

Dates

North Springs High School (Visual Arts Magnet) • Atlanta, GA

2002 - present

- Senior, GPA 3.4
- Honors classes: Algebra II, Pre-Calculus, Physics, 10th-grade Lit, American Lit, Bio Chemistry, Organic Chemistry, Economics, Spanish IV, Spanish Culture
- AP classes: Spanish, Computer Science, Psychology, Environmental Science, Art Portolio, Art 2-D Design, U.S. History
- Will be receiving the Georgia High School College Preparatory Diploma with Distinction with the Visual and Performing Arts —Math/Science Magnet Seal

College

Will be attending Amherst College in the fall of 2006, majoring in Fine Arts, Psychology, and Black Studies.

Experience

Rising Sun Publishing • Marietta, GA

2001 - present

Designer: Responsible for assisting in the layout and design of the company catalog, packing and preparing bookorders for shipment, answering the telephone, and uploading and stocking book shipments.

Tommy Cho Karate • Marietta, GA

2002 - present

Assistant Karate Instructor: Responsible for working with youth and adults. Provide training in the forms of Martial Arts.

Was also responsible for opening school and preparing for birthday parties, providing Martial Arts demonstration for youth birthday celebrations.

North Springs High School • Atlanta, GA

North Springs High School Touchdown Club: Assisted with the layout and design of the annual football program and web site maintenance. Responsibilities included working with desktop publishing software, photographic touch up using Adobe Photoshop, and uploading data files to the NSHS web site.

Skills

Proficient in Spanish.
Good organization, communication, and interpersonal skills.
Have worked on both Macintosh and PCs. Familiar with Microsoft Word, Adobe Photoshop, Adobe Illustrator, Adobe Elements, QuarkXPress, InDesign, Powerpoint, and Keynote.
Familiar with web site design, Java, and HTML programming.

Activities

Varsity Football	2003 - present
Varsity Track and Field	2002 - present
Lacrosse	2005 - present
Martial Arts Instructor	2002 - present
Youth Basketball Coach	2002 - 03

Awards

Who's Who Among America's High School Students	2004
National Honor Roll	2004
Super Honor Roll, Principal's List, Honor Roll	2002 - present
Varsity Football Letter (2)	2003 - 04
Varsity Track Letter (2)	2003 - 04
Varsity Lacrosse Letter (2)	2005 - 06
Atlanta Hawks Black History Month Art Contest Finalist	2003
Black Belt in Ho Shin Do Martial Arts	1995

References available upon request

Job or Activity   **Dates of involvement**

_____

_____

Description of my involvement:

_____

_____

Description of leadership skills developed or offices obtained:

_____

_____

_____

_____

What I learned from my involvement:

_____

_____

_____

_____

_____

Why this activity had a special significance for me:

_____

_____

_____

_____

_____

_____

Future involvement that I anticipate in this activity during or after college:

_____

_____

_____

_____

_____
_____
_____
_____
_____

Education   **Dates**

_____   _____
_____   _____
_____   _____

Objective

_____   _____
_____   _____

Experience

_____   _____
_____   _____
_____   _____
_____   _____
_____   _____
_____   _____
_____   _____
_____   _____

Skills

_____   _____
_____   _____
_____   _____
_____   _____

Activities

_____   _____
_____   _____
_____   _____
_____   _____

Awards

_____   _____
_____   _____
_____   _____
_____   _____

References available upon request

Know the facts

If you are a top athlete, you may find yourself becoming a recruited-athlete. This may open opportunities to be admitted into top colleges and universities, however, be mindful that an athletic scholarship is more likely to provide an opportunity for a college education than pave the way to a career in professional sports.

Estimated Probability of Competing in Athletics Beyond High School

Source: http://www.ncaa.org/research/prob_of_competing/

Student-Athletes	Men's Basketball	Women's Basketball	Football	Baseball	Men's Ice Hockey	Men's Soccer
High School Student-Athletes	549,500	456,900	983,600	455,300	29,900	321,400
High School Senior Student-Athletes	157,000	130,500	281,000	130,100	8,500	91,800
NCAA Student-Athletes	15,700	14,400	56,500	25,700	3,700	18,200
NCAA Freshman Roster Positions	4,500	4,100	16,200	7,300	1,100	5,200
NCAA Senior Student-Athletes	3,500	3,200	12,600	5,700	800	4,100
NCAA Student-Athletes Drafted	44	32	250	600	33	76
Percent High School to NCAA	2.9	3.1	5.8	5.6	12.9	5.7
Percent NCAA to Professional	1.3	1.0	2.0	10.5	4.1	1.9
Percent High School to Professional	0.03[1]	0.02	0.09[2]	0.5	0.4	0.08

1. Players must be at least 19 years old and out of high school one year to be eligible for the NBA draft.
2. Players must be at out of high school three years to be eligible for the NFL draft.

Related facts:

- Only 3 out of every 100 high school basketball players will play college basketball.
- Only 8 out of every 100,000 will be drafted into the NBA/WNBA.
- Only 6 out of every 100 high school football players will play college football.
- Only 25 out of every 100,000 will be drafted into the NFL.

Section III

Honesty
Integrity
Justice
Resilience

Personal Qualities

Academic achievement is really only one factor in admissions; the college is also looking for integrity, maturity, initiative and, above all, creativity. No college wants to be boring! Your application is a sales package, and your 'hook' is your uniqueness. What makes you a superstar? Something does, I guarantee it. A good college counselor can find it. Your parents may know what it is. But something unique is within you, waiting to be brought out, developed, and packaged for colleges to consider. Do not try to tell a college that you are good at everything; tell them you are great at something.

— *[College Admissions Trade Secrets]*

Personal Qualities

❑ Leadership
❑ Character

Leadership

Your participation in athletic and academic competitions, leadership programs, trips to other parts of the country or the world, building a science model, or building a business will add to your unique set of experiences.

 *Refer to page 166 for a complete listing of summer camp opportunities and academic enrichment programs.*

 *Avoid discipline infractions. One of the first questions that many colleges ask, "Have you ever been suspended from school?" Do not give them a reason to deny your application (see page 155).*

Identify camps, internships, and enrichment programs, and note the qualifying criteria (e.g., participation in certain clubs, enrollment in certain classes, or recommendation by teachers or counselors). Go to *www.accessandequity.org* for a listing of programs and links to other web sites.

Colleges are looking for leaders—students who can contribute to intellectual discussions, challenge professors, create music, explore science, provide creative and intellectual insight into the issues of today and contribute to their communities.

Identify the offices or leadership positions in which you are interested. Share your goals with your counselor, teachers, and coaches to ensure that the leadership positions in which you are interested can be achieved and the likely year of school that you will be able to achieve your desired position.

Identify each activity and desired position, office, or leadership role:

Activity   **Desired Position or Office**

_____

_____

_____

_____

_____

_____

There are many opportunities to develop or demonstrate leadership skills. Review the following and check all that apply. Describe your experiences on the following page.

❑ I contributed to the creation of a student club or organization.

❑ I started a business.

❑ I have been elected into office or served in a leadership capacity in an organization.

❑ I served as the captain or co-captain of an athletic team.

❑ I served on the student council or in student government.

❑ I created a new approach or implemented a new way of doing things that has enhanced my school, organization, or community.

❑ I taught or tutored a subject or activity.

❑ I coached or mentored others.

❑ I took something that I learned through a classroom experience and applied it to the creation of a new product or new way of doing things.

❑ I wrote, illustrated, or published a book.

❑ I wrote, directed, or had a leading role in a play.

❑ I wrote or recorded a song.

❑ I choreographed or performed a dance routine.

❑ I have been publicly recognized for heroism or leadership.

❑ I developed a web site.

❑ I led an effort to change something in my school or community.

Description of what you did, when you did it, and the leadership skills you developed:

_____

_____

_____

_____

_____

_____

_____

_____

_____

_____

_____

_____

_____

Demonstrating leadership skills may increase your chances of being admitted to top colleges:

The already crazed competition for admission to the nation's most prestigious universities and colleges became even more intense this year, with many logging record low acceptance rates.

Harvard College, for example, offered admission to only 7.1 percent of the 27,462 high school seniors who applied—or, put another way, it rejected 93 of every 100 applicants, many with extraordinary achievements, like a perfect score on one of the SAT exams. Yale College accepted 8.3 percent of its 22,813 applicants. Both rates were records.

— *[April 1, 2008, New York Times*
Elite Colleges Reporting Record Lows in Admission]

Character

Your character defines who you are, what you stand for, and the beliefs and principles that you live by. Do not allow yourself to be influenced by mean-spirited, self-centered, obnoxious people who go out of their way to ridicule, take advantage of, and hinder others. Do not follow the crowd or allow such people to define your character.

What are your values, beliefs, and guiding principles? Ultimately, a person will be known by his or her works. Whatever the values that truly define who you are in the 9th grade, they will be evident in your works by the time you write your college essays in the 11th and 12th grades.

Look over the words and phrases on the following list and circle those that reflect your character or your beliefs:

Integrity	Perseverance	Diligent	Compassionate
Fair	Excellence	Honest	Responsible
Intense	Passionate	Fortitude	Self-starter
Resilient	Spiritual	Dependable	Principled
Introspective	Determined	Focused	Leader
Collaborative	Sense of justice	Respectful	Team Player
Quality	Thoughtful	Creative	Self-motivated
Cooperative	Pensive	Confident	Assertive
Considerate	Initiative	Respectful	Resolute
Courageous	Persistent	Conviction	Resourceful

What additional words or phrases define your character and beliefs?

_____

_____

_____

_____

What are your gifts?

An important part of your high school experience will be to maximize your gifts. However, before you can maximize your gifts you must know what they are. List your gifts in such areas as:

Academics • Athletics • Creative • Personal • Leadership

_____

_____

_____

_____

_____

_____

_____

_____

_____

_____

_____

_____

_____

_____

_____

_____

_____

Section IV

Intangibles

Summer is your child's chance to win the edge, to beat the competition. The most important time for out-of-school enrichment is summer—when many opportunities exist to explore and develop interests. By fall, your son or daughter should possess an entirely new repertoire of abilities. Anything else is a waste.

Colleges ask on the applications what the applicant did every summer starting with the summer before ninth grade. This section should be filled with many exciting adventures, challenges, experiences, and extra learning that the high schools don't offer.

— [What Colleges Don't Tell You and Other Parents Don't Want You to Know]

Intangibles

❑ Personal Profile
❑ Summer Programs
❑ Essay

What's your story?

Colleges attempt to create a diverse class of students. They look for differences in race, gender, geographical location, socioeconomic backgrounds, culture, and communities. They hope to cultivate enriching classroom experiences that reflect diverse ideas and opinions.

Your college application and your essay provide the opportunity to share your story and to celebrate your uniqueness. What are your hopes, your dreams, your struggles, and your triumphs?

What is special and unique about you?

Celebrate your uniqueness

Your intangibles reflect all of the things that make you different. The more you are different from the thousands of other applicants the greater your chances of being accepted into the most competitive schools.

Some of the criteria that make up your intangibles are:

- ❑ Legacy student
- ❑ First generation to attend college
- ❑ Race
- ❑ Gender
- ❑ Speak multiple languages
- ❑ Top academic student
- ❑ Top athlete
- ❑ Created new student club/organization
- ❑ Winner of prestigious competition
- ❑ Geographical location
- ❑ Team captain/officer in student organization
- ❑ Recognized for volunteer work
- ❑ Recognized for artistic or creative achievement
- ❑ Recognized for heroism
- ❑ Socioeconomic background
- ❑ Program director, counselor, tutor, or coach
- ❑ Martial arts instructor
- ❑ Overcame unique family tragedy
- ❑ Unique summer camp or travel experiences

My Profile

Race/Gender: **Legacy Student?**

_____

Where I Currently Live:

_____

Other Places I Have Lived:

_____

_____

Languages I Speak Fluently:

_____

Obstacles I Have Overcome:

_____

_____

Major Awards or Accomplishments:

_____

_____

Unique Experiences:

_____

_____

Things I am Passionate About:

_____

_____

Leadership Abilities I Have Demonstrated:

_____

_____

Maximize your summers

The summer months between 8th grade and your senior year of high school should not be squandered. Take advantage of the many opportunities to explore your talents, interests, and abilities. Consider the following opportunities. Place a check next to those you would have an opportunity to do:

- ❏ Travel
- ❏ Work in a meaningful job related to an area of interest or an internship
- ❏ Participate in a summer learning experience through an academic, artistic, or community service opportunity
- ❏ Participate in a pre-college program or summer camp
- ❏ Participate in an AAU, USATF, or club sport
- ❏ Participate in summer practice for a high school sport such as football, cross country, lacrosse, soccer, swimming, etc.
- ❏ Volunteer or work as a counselor, life guard, coach, or art instructor at a parks and recreation, Boys & Girls Club, or community program
- ❏ Take non-academic classes or electives in summer school to allow for more honors or advanced classes during the regular school year
- ❏ Start a business or work on a special project
- ❏ Write a book, compose music, or choreograph a dance routine

Your passionate areas of interest contribute to your uniqueness and may enhance the diversity of a college community. Do you teach martial arts? Do you coach little league baseball? Do you run a soccer clinic for inner-city youth during the summer? Do you volunteer for political campaigns? Are you a tutor in a literacy program at the Boys & Girls Club? Such programs, involvement, and areas of interest help to shape your uniqueness.

Align your areas of interest with a college major. Use your research to assess the college's commitment to your field of study and its student diversity needs. For example, female students interested in pursuing such majors as engineering, mathematics, or science, which typically have fewer female applicants, may find themselves more aggressively recruited than female students interested in pursuing nursing, which has a large number of female applicants.

[Taken from, "A High School Plan for Students with College-Bound Dreams," p. 162]

Refer to page 166 for a listing of popular summer programs.

While you have little control over gender, race, or the socioeconomic level of your family, participating in a wide range of summer programs can greatly enhance your intangibles. Art, science, math, foreign language immersion, acting, athletics, marine biology, internships, entrepreneurship, and pre-college programs are available throughout the country. Programs may be offered by your local school district, universities, community colleges, youth organizations, or community agencies. Finding out about such programs is just a click away—google, "Summer Programs" and you are on your way. The best programs quickly fill so you should do your research in the fall and register for summer programs as early as January. Go to *www.accessandequity.org* for a listing of summer programs and links to other web sites.

Do not miss out on college opportunities, talk to your counselor:

Jennie, a Chicago-born Latina, is an extremely bright, hardworking student who completed a rigorous IB program; was a candidate for 12-year perfect attendance; GPA of 3.84; 21 on the ACT; and was involved in cheerleading, drama, science club, debate team, and the National Honor Society.

Managing the college search process left Jennie feeling overwhelmed and confused. In her senior year, Jennie's college search never really got off the ground. Her college application activities were unfocused and disorganized. Jennie never spoke one-on-one with a teacher or counselor about her college plans.

— *[From High School to the Future: Potholes on the Road to College]*

Identify the camps, pre-college programs, or activities you will participate in during each summer following the end of each grade level:

8th Grade _____

_____

_____

_____

_____

9th Grade _____

_____

_____

_____

_____

10th Grade _____

_____

_____

_____

_____

11th Grade _____

_____

_____

_____

_____

Start working on your essay

Few students want to write their application or scholarship essays so they put them off until the last minute. By so doing, they create poorly written essays, filled with mistakes, and in essence sabotage their own applications. If you begin early (ideally by ninth grade) and develop your writing skills slowly and deliberately, you can become a good writer and develop a great essay.

 *Review Chapter 11, "Your Essay" (p. 175) for the do's and don'ts of essay writing.*

Select a topic from the following list and write an essay on the following page. Choose a different topic each week and have someone review them with you:

❏ Hard work

❏ Overcoming obstacles

❏ Being of service

❏ Teamwork

❏ Perseverance

❏ Individual initiative

❏ Passion and enthusiasm

❏ Responsibility

❏ Civic duty

❏ Purpose

❏ Character or core value

❏ Autobiography

❏ Person you most admire

❏ Major challenge in your life

❏ Something significant that you want to accomplish

❏ Your strengths and weaknesses

❏ An issue of personal, local, national, or international concern

❏ Actions you would take if you were in a position of leadership, e.g., politician, principal, CEO, etc.

Formatting Your Essay

Pay close attention to the guidelines for formatting, number of words, content, or theme of your essay based on published admissions or scholarship guidelines.

• Double-space

• Use a common twelve-point font (etc., Times, Times New Roman, Helvetica)

• Set margins from 1 to 1 1/4" from the sides and 1" from the top and bottom

• Follow the APA (American Psychological Association) format for your title page, header, and footer

• Staple securely in the upper left-hand corner

• Develop a title that captures the reader's attention, e.g., "Do Students Dare to Rise Above Mediocrity?" will catch your reader's attention more than "Kids are Lazy."

• Place page numbers in the footer

• Make the appropriate footnotes, references, and citations

_____

_____

_____

_____

_____

_____

_____

_____

_____

_____

_____

_____

_____

_____

_____

Do not take your essay lightly; it may represent the most important part of your entire application package. It will provide you an opportunity to define who you are and state your case for admission into the college to which you are applying. It can take away from or enhance the overall picture of who you are, what you stand for, and why the admissions committee should give you an opportunity ahead of the thousands of other applicants. This is your opportunity to explain your grades; share your convictions, beliefs, philosophies, and guiding principles; tell what you know about the college's values, beliefs, and traditions; and merge your hopes, dreams, and aspirations.

[Taken from, "A High School Plan for Students with College-Bound Dreams," p. 175]

Principles, Values, and Ideals that should be reflected in your essay

Your essay should make an impression on the reader. In essence, your essay represents a voice in the room that is speaking on your behalf. The principles, values, and ideals that your essay communicates will help to describe what you believe, define who you are, and present a case for why you have qualities that should be highly valued by the colleges that you apply to.

Passion	Purpose	Perseverance	Integrity
Diligence	Determination	Persistence	Dedication
Devotion	Commitment	Enthusiasm	Energy
Fortitude	Kindness	Humanity	Generosity
Selflessness	Tolerance	Awareness	Service
Leadership	Teamwork	Cooperation	Humor
Originality	Innovation	Imagination	Thoughtful
Judgment	Independence	Honor	Morality
Resilience	Experimentation	Idealism	Vision
Mission	Conceptualized	Created	Explored
Pursued	Discovered	Developed	Taught
Trained	Coached	Coordinated	Reformed
Respect	Responsibility	Established	Initiated
Compassion	Inspired	Founded	Tutored
Sense of duty	Collaborated	Led	Mission
Entrepreneurship	Moral responsibility	Citizenship	Pursued

Use your essay to tell your story

Imagine your essay standing on a stage. The curtain pulls back and your essay walks from center stage to the podium. The spotlight shines, but there is talking and lack of interest throughout the room as thousands of other essays whisper, motion, and scream for attention, yet it is your essay standing alone at the podium as a Sunday morning preacher.

There is silence throughout the auditorium as all voices and distractions quiet. All discourse, debate, and discussions become still as a lake beneath the moonlight, as your essay captures, captivates, and presents a brilliant oratory on your behalf—sharing your hopes and your dreams, your achievements and your aspirations, your frailties and your uniqueness—your essay is the single ripple on the water carrying your message as the ripples widen and spread into the spirit, soul, and consciousness of the listener.

Heroes and Heroines

As your leadership skills, character, core values, and guiding principles provide the intangibles that define who you are, so too will your heroes and heroines. Are your heroes and heroines hip hop, rap, or pop stars? Are you a groupie who admires and follows entertainers and athletes? Are those whom you most admire likely to reflect the core values and character traits that you value and which, ultimately, define who you are or who you aspire to become?

Some of the questions to be answered are:

- What stories have I read of leadership, personal sacrifice, or service that have inspired me?

- What people have demonstrated, through their lives or their ability to overcome obstacles, an example that I wish to follow?

- What people have left a legacy that has provided an example of the values that humanity should aspire toward?

- What people embody the values, beliefs, and ideals that define who I am or what I aspire to become?

- What people have, through their thoughts, words, or deeds, changed the course of human history in a meaningful and relevant way?

- With which historical figures would I value the opportunity to sit and discuss ideas, opinions, and views on the most pressing social or political issues of the day?

Make a list of the people whom you most admire in such areas as:

- Family or community

- Historical figures

- Political, civic, business, or religious leaders

- Educators (i.e., teachers, counselors, administrators, or coaches)

- Athletes, entertainers, and public figures

- Everyday people, e.g., custodians, cafeteria workers, farmers, brick masons, waiters or waitresses

[Taken from, "A High School Plan for Students with College-Bound Dreams," p. 180]

Section V
Application &
Financial Aid

The 1998-1999 application season was the most competitive in U.S. history, with the best colleges reporting extremely low admit rates. Just to name a few, Harvard and Princeton admitted 11 percent of their applicants; Columbia, 14 percent; Stanford, 15 percent; Amherst, 19 percent; and Swarthmore, 21 percent. Those excluded from these small percentages of admitted students include many highly qualified applicants who believed they were likely or certain to do well in the college application process because their numbers and scores looked just like those of the fortunate few who got in.

— *[How to Get in to the Top Colleges]*

Financial Aid

❑ Financial-aid Checklist
❑ Application Package Checklist
❑ Senior-Year To Do List

Financial-aid Checklist

❑ **Step 1: Set aside two boxes**

Set aside two boxes for your scholarship information:

❑ One box for the scholarships that you apply to which will contain your essays and necessary application information

❑ The second box for your overflow of scholarship information that you may not be considering at this time

❑ **Step 2: Get a reliable mailing address**

You are going to begin receiving lots of mail. You need a stable address for the next FOUR years! If your family moves around a lot consider getting a P.O. Box or using the address of a family member who is stable (e.g., grandparents). **This includes a permanent e-mail address.**

❑ **Step 3: Get a high speed Internet connection**

Researching and downloading scholarship and college information will require a high speed Internet connection. If you do not have access to a high speed connection at home then plan to spend time before and after school using the computers in the school's library, media center, or computer lab.

❑ **Step 4: Get your paperwork together**

Get your essays and paperwork together. Keep all of your original documents filed neatly in your box and keep copies in your binder under the appropriate tabs like grades, test scores, transcript, letters of recommendation, financial records, awards, essays, summaries of your extracurricular activities, etc.

❑ **Step 5: Fill out the necessary forms**

Gather together all of the mandatory forms—tax forms, social security numbers, employment income, assets, liabilities, etc.

❏ Step 6: Identify your niche

Identify the scholarship opportunities that are unique to your race, gender, activities, community, and state.

Refer to Chapter 12, "Financial Aid/ Scholarships" (p. 188) for complete information regarding FAFSA, the Common Application, and deadlines for applying for financial aid.

❏ Step 7: Establish a research schedule

Identify when you will do research, how you will organize yourself, and how you will ensure that you complete the packages and send them off by the deadline.

❏ Step 8: Package yourself

Carefully research the large scholarships. Understand the organization's philosophy and its ideal scholarship recipient, and package yourself to be that recipient. Write the essay that the scholarship committee needs to hear, highlight the achievements that they think important, and get letters of recommendations from the type of people whom they value. Make them want to give you the scholarship.

❏ Step 9: Establish a submission schedule

Plan to submit applications at specific intervals, e.g., weekly, bi-monthly, monthly, every other month, etc.

❏ Step 10: Identify the available local, state, and federal financial-aid sources

Meet with your counselor and identify all of the local financial-aid sources.

❏ Step 11: Apply, apply, apply

Do not apply for a few big ones; instead, apply for as many as you can, as often as you can.

❑ **Step 12: Do not pay entry fees**

There are too many scholarships to waste your time and money paying entry fees for a chance to win back your money.

❑ **Step 13: Share your information**

The best way to inspire people to share their information with you is to approach them first with information. Tell your friends about the scholarships you find out about.

❑ **Step 14: Keep that winning essay**

Despite researching and referring to all the essay-writing books, you do not know that you have written a winning essay until the check is in the mail. Do not throw away any of your essays, even the ones that you think are badly written.

❑ **Step 15: Develop a relationship with your counselor**

If you successfully win a *scholarship*, go back to your counselor and personally let him or her know how much you won and how much you appreciate his or her help.

❑ **Step 16: Follow instructions**

Follow instructions and meet deadlines!

Service-Cancelable Loans

Explore the opportunities for service-cancelable loans to assist in financing your college education. These loans may allow you to earn a salary while repaying your education loan after graduating from college or they may be forgiven entirely if you work for a certain number of years in an area related to your education and recognized as an area of critical need in your state (e.g., education, health care, social services, etc.).

These types of loans may be available based on fields of study, military service, law enforcement, or teaching.

Speak to your counselor or contact your state department of education to identify the available service-cancelable loans.

Acquiring the needed financial aid to pay for the cost of college can be as simple as meeting state qualifying standards (such as obtaining a 3.0 GPA in a Georgia high school and qualifying for Georgia's Hope Scholarship to be used at Georgia colleges), as time-consuming as combing through the many scholarship books and web sites, or simply paying private scholarship consultants. Putting together your financial-aid treasure chest will require that you determine the best strategy for you based on your family's needs and your top-ten list of colleges.

[Taken from, "A High School Plan for Students with College-Bound Dreams," p. 188]

Application Package

Carefully read Chapter 13 "Your Application Package." On the following pages is a checklist of some of the important deadlines and decisions. You can have a great high school plan, only to blow it by submitting your application late, forgetting to enclose all of the requested forms, or by making any number of the common mistakes, i.e., misspellings, incorrect word usage, or sending the application to the wrong school! Take your time and have someone double check that everything is correctly and properly done.

Refer to Chapter 13, "Your Application Package" (p. 199) for information regarding the types of admissions cycles.

Application Checklist

❑ Decide whether or not you will be required to take SAT IIs and schedule them as soon as possible following the end of the course (e.g., Algebra, History, Spanish, etc.)

❑ Identify and notify people whom you want to write letters of recommendation

❑ Complete all of the worksheets in this book with all of the necessary information to complete your college applications

❑ Identify a permanent mailing address, e-mail address, and phone number

❑ Have checks, money orders, or fee waivers for all of the schools you plan to apply to

❑ Prepare a transcript request form for each school

❑ Choose the admissions cycle you will apply to

❑ Decide whether to use the Common Application

❑ Complete any supplements (e.g., art, music, athletics)

❑ Prepare for interviews if required

❑ Have access to a computer or typewriter to complete applications

❑ Organize a folder or envelope to keep copies of the applications to each school

❑ Gather all of the necessary forms to complete the FAFSA and CSS Profile (if required)

Get an Application Fee Waiver

There are many ways to save the application fees, which can amount to hundreds of dollars if a student is applying to several colleges:

- *Demonstrate financial need.*

- *Submit the application through a college fair where many schools waive the application fee.*

- *Begin contacting the college. Oftentimes colleges will send prospective students fee waivers.*

- *Ask for one!*

Senior Year

Your senior year will contain many important dates and deadlines. It is imperative that you organize yourself. You must know where your information is, you must keep track of important dates and deadlines, and stay focused. The first three years of high school have prepared you for and led you to this point. You should have performed your research, done your college visits, and prepared your essays. You should already have arranged your list of top-ten schools into chronological order. The only thing that should cause you to change your mind at this point is an offer package from a school that was not on your list—an offer that is so good that you must give the school and the package serious consideration.

What you have sown will determine the strength of your application package, which will influence the college admissions cycle that you choose to use. Some of the groups in which you may find yourself include:

- *Academic Superstar:* Your grades, course work, and standardized test scores have elevated you to the level of "Academic Superstar." You may have received a number of merit-based scholarships and find yourself a recruited student who has many college options. Hopefully, one or more of your options are schools that you have noted on your top-ten list.

- *Recruited-athlete:* Your success within one or more varsity sports has qualified you as a recruited-athlete. You may have already received offers via the National Letter of Intent program and now find yourself going through the difficult task of evaluating schools and offers. Hopefully, you have received scholarship offers from some of the schools on your top-ten list or are in a position to use offer letters from other schools to negotiate a financial-aid package with the schools on your list.

- *Strong Candidate:* The success that you have achieved within one or more of the areas (i.e., academics, extracurricular activities, etc.) makes you a strong candidate for admissions. While your acceptance is not guaranteed, you may feel that you are a strong enough candidate who is likely to receive enough acceptance letters that you will be able to compare financial-aid packages prior to committing to a particular college.

- *Legacy Student:* Regardless of whether you are an academic superstar, recruited-athlete, or strong candidate you have made up your mind and are committed to apply under the guidelines as a legacy applicant.

- *Weak Candidate:* After reviewing your application package, you realize that you are not a stand-out student in any area. However, if you are serious about going to college, then you, more than any other student, will have to do some research. Identify schools where you meet their minimum requirements, particularly schools with open enrollment policies, and you must take the time to put together a quality application package and meet all of their posted deadlines. NO EXCEPTIONS!

[Taken from, "A High School Plan for Students with College-Bound Dreams," p. 200]

Organize your information so that everything you need is readily available as you complete and submit your paperwork in accordance with the following deadlines.

Important web sites:

- AP Program *(www.apcentral.collegeboard.com)*
- FAFSA *(www.fafsa.ed.gov)*
- Common Application *(www.commonapp.org)*
- Compare Colleges *(www.collegeresults.org; www.ucan-network.org/)*
- Foundation for Ensuring Access and Equity *(www.accessandequity.org)*
- ACT *(www.actstudent.org)*
- SAT *(www.collegeboard.com)*

July/August

❑ Complete a preliminary FAFSA and CSS Profile. Identify the information that you and your parents must still acquire, i.e., W2 forms, estimated income, bank statements, etc. Set up a calendar to gather together all of the necessary information by December 31.

❑ Review your SAT I/ACT scores and decide whether or not to take either or both again. If so, register for the fall exams.

❑ Review the information that you have gathered from your top-ten list of schools. Make sure you have completed a draft application for each school and make any final request for information, e.g., brochures, financial-aid forms, etc.

❑ Carefully review each of your desired schools' SAT II requirements and register for any needed SAT II exams.

❑ Organize your scholarship essays.

❑ Count your money. How much financial aid have you gathered thus far? Continue identifying financial-aid and scholarship opportunities and continue submitting essays and applications.

❑ Organize your college admission essays for each school you are applying to.

❑ Review your transcript. How many credits and core requirements will you need to pass during your senior year? If you are planning to enroll as a student-athlete, compare your transcript against the NCAA Clearinghouse guidelines and eligibility requirements (www.ncaastudent.org).

❑ If you are a student-athlete and you have not done so, register with the NCAA Clearinghouse.

❑ Meet with your counselor to confirm that you have taken the necessary courses thus far and that your senior-year schedule will meet the graduation requirements in your high school and admissions requirements for the colleges to which you are applying.

❑ Confirm that you have passed all of the required exit exams and schedule test dates for those exams you have not passed.

❑ Review with your counselor such issues as guidelines for transcripts, recommendations, how long to allow for counselor recommendations, etc. Get any needed request forms and attach to each of your application folders.

❑ Get a wall or desk calendar and write down all the dates and deadlines relating to admissions (i.e., Early Action, Regular, Rolling, etc.) and financial aid (i.e., application deadlines, FAFSA filing, merit scholarships, etc.), so that you do not miss any dates or deadlines.

September

❑ Early September is the registration deadline for the October SAT I.

❑ Schedule college interviews.

❑ Request your final letters of recommendation from teachers, advisors, employers, coaches, counselors, etc.

October

❑ Submit Early Admissions or Early Action applications.

❑ Request transcripts for each of your application packages.

❑ Review your preliminary FAFSA and CSS Profile for early admissions consideration.

November

❑ Ensure that your SAT I, SAT II, and ACT scores are sent to your college choices.

❑ Update your résumé, bio, or admissions package with your new extracurricular activities, awards, community service, etc.

❑ Begin preparing for college or scholarship interviews.

December

❏ If you applied under the Early Decision guidelines you should be receiving a response from your Early Decision school. If you are accepted, move forward with setting up your calendar to meet all requested deadlines and requirements for your financial-aid package. If you were not accepted, continue with your plan for further consideration at this school and for submitting your application packages to your other choices.

❏ Complete your final college applications and prepare your FAFSA forms. Make sure that you and your parents/guardian file a copy of your final pay stubs, 1099s, and W2 forms and complete your income calculations.

❏ Confirm your important senior-year dates, i.e., ordering your cap and gown, graduation practice, senior rings, etc.

January

❏ Submit your FAFSA as soon as possible after January 1. Set up a FAFSA folder. You will have to complete the FAFSA for each year that you attend college and apply for financial aid. WRITE DOWN YOUR PIN AND PASSWORD.

❏ Complete all college financial-aid forms and keep copies for your records.

❏ Send required mid-year reports to colleges.

❏ Verify that all your applications have been received.

❏ Request your mid-year transcript and place a copy into your file.

February

❏ Approximately four weeks after submitting your FAFSA, you should receive your SAR. Review it for accuracy and immediately correct any errors. Write your DRN down onto your college worksheets and file a copy in each applications folder (this way it will be nearly impossible for it to get lost).

March

❏ You still have one more chance to take the SAT! This month is the final deadline for late registration.

❏ Start planning for a summer job or internship so you can earn money for your first year of college.

April

❑ Most *regular admissions* decisions and financial-aid packages will arrive this month.

❑ Review your financial-aid packages and pay attention to response deadlines and requests for additional information.

❑ If you are wait listed by any college, contact the admissions office to reaffirm your desire to attend.

May

❑ Final AP exams and SAT IIs. Have your scores sent to the college or university where you plan to enroll.

❑ Send thank you notes to teachers, counselors, coaches, and others who wrote recommendation letters, assisted you in preparing your application packages, or provided financial assistance; and to scholarship programs to both thank and advise them of your final college choice.

❑ Notify (in writing) the colleges you have decided not to attend.

❑ Ensure that you have received all necessary forms from the college you plan to attend (i.e., financial aid, housing, health insurance, etc.).

June

❑ Have your final transcript sent to your college.

❑ Get a jump start on setting up your bank accounts, wire transfer requirements, etc., near your college.

❑ Set up your first-year budget.

July/August

❑ Notify the financial-aid office of your college about any scholarships you have been offered.

Start packing.

APPENDIX I

COLLEGE LITERACY QUIZ
ANSWER KEY

College Literacy Quiz (p. 2) Answer Key

1. What are AP and IB courses?

   Advanced Placement and International Baccalaureate.

2. When are AP exams given and what scores typically qualify for college credit?

   May; Scores of 3 - 5.

3. Who administers the AP and IB Programs?

   AP: College Board; IB: International Baccalaureate Organization.

4. What does the 'weight,' of such classes mean?

   Additional points added to a student's GPA.

5. Is the Ivy League an athletic or academic grouping of colleges?

   Athletic Conference.

6. How many colleges make up the Ivy League?

   Eight; Brown, Columbia, Cornell, Dartmouth, Harvard, Penn, Princeton, and Yale

7. What does HBCU stand for?

   Historically Black Colleges and Universities.

8. How many HBCUs are there?

   90 4-year and 13 2-year colleges and universities (source: U.S. Department of Education [http://www.ed.gov/about/inits/list/whhbcu/edlite-list.html]).

9. What is the difference between the SAT I, SAT II, and the ACT and what is the top score for each exam?

   SAT I tests reasoning (top scores are 800 for each section—Math, Critical Reading, and Writing— resulting in a combined top score of 2400); SAT II are subject tests (top scores are 800); ACT tests a student's subject knowledge (top score is 36).

10. How many times can you take the SAT I and ACT?

    Unlimited.

11. Which type of high school classes will best prepare you for success on the Critical Reading and Writing Sections of the SAT I?

    English, language arts, history, philosophy.

12. What advantage, if any, is there to taking the SAT I or ACT more than once?

You can combine your highest SAT I scores from different tests (i.e., Math, Critical Reading, Writing) and you can increase your ACT score.

13. What is the PSAT and in which grade (i.e., 9th, 10th, 11th, or 12th) do the scores qualify students as National Merit and National Achievement Scholars?

Preliminary SAT I; 11th-grade scores.

14. What does GPA mean?

Grade Point Average.

15. What is a weighted GPA?

GPA plus any additional points from honors, AP, IB or other advanced classes.

16. With what organization does a college-bound athlete have to register?

NCAA Clearinghouse.

17. What is the significance of taking classes for high school credit while in middle school?

Counts towards your high school credit requirements and allows a student to take the next level of classes (i.e., Spanish II, Algebra II, etc.).

18. What is joint or dual enrollment?

Enrollment in both high school and college classes.

19. What is the significance of taking advanced math classes in middle school?

Access to a higher level of high school math (i.e., Algebra II, Geometry, Pre-Calculus, Calculus).

20. What is the most important academic skill that colleges want incoming students to demonstrate?

Communication.

21. Does a student from a top private school have a significantly better chance of being admitted to college over a student from an average public high school?

No. Students are usually compared against other students from similar backgrounds and schools.

22. What are complimentary sports and how can they increase your college admissions opportunities?

Sports that utilize or develop a similar set of skills, e.g., football–lacrosse, football–track and field, baseball–basketball, etc.

23. Will being a top academic achiever and having high SAT I/ACT scores guarantee that you will be accepted into the college of your choice?

No. Academic achievement and SAT I/ACT scores are only part of the admissions criteria.

24. Will average grades and average SAT I/ACT scores guarantee that you will not be accepted into the college of your choice?

No. Academic achievement and SAT I/ACT scores are only part of the admissions criteria.

25. Who is a legacy student?

A student whose parents graduated from the college's undergraduate program.

26. What is FAFSA, why is it important, and when should you complete it?

Free Application for Federal Student Aid; determines a student's financial need; and should be completed as soon as possible after January 1 of the year that you will be enrolling in college. Must also be completed each year that you are attending college and applying for financial aid.

27. What is EFC?

Expected Family Contribution.

28. What is Need-based—Need-blind admissions?

Admissions does not take into account student financial need, however, the student's financial-aid package is based on student need.

29. What is an articulation agreement?

An agreement between schools, typically a two-year college that allows ease of transfer into a four-year university.

30. How many colleges can a student apply to under the Early Decision program?

One.

Why should I care? (p. 7) Answer Key

1. What are the course requirements for admissions into the state universities in your state?

   See page 49 in the book.

2. Are high school exit or graduation exams given in your school district? If so, what are they?

   See page 50 in the book.

3. Is there an advantage to declaring a college major? If you answer 'Yes' explain.

   See page 62 in the book.

4. What is a high school profile and why do colleges request them?

   See page 62 in the book.

5. What is the significance of class rank in your state university system? What about private or competitive colleges?

   See page 80 in the book.

6. How many, and what type of diplomas can you receive from your high school?

   See page 47 in the book.

7. Can an athlete graduate from high school and still be ineligible to compete in college? If you answer 'Yes' explain why.

   See page 52 in the book.

8. Can an athlete with a 4.0 GPA still be declared ineligible by the NCAA Clearinghouse?

   See page 52 in the book.

9. Can a student with a 4.0 GPA still be denied admission into a state university?

   See page 49 in the book.

10. Can a student with average grades and average SAT or ACT scores, be admitted into a highly-competitive college?

    See page 27 in the book.

What Admissions Committees Look For

When you submit your college application packages, you will be submitting your information along with thousands of other students from throughout the country, and depending on the colleges to which you apply, from throughout the world. Colleges will be looking for a diverse student body; hence, their admissions criteria will reflect a number of components: grades, test scores, types of classes, activities, interests, student backgrounds, community service, and any number of other criteria unique to the needs of the college or university to which you apply. Your high school transcript will reflect not only your academic success in high school, but also your willingness to be challenged and your areas of interest. The type of classes—math, science, language arts, social studies, and electives—and the level of those classes—honors, AP, IB—will be considered along with your grades.

[Taken from, "A High School Plan for Students with College-Bound Dreams," p. 58]

Do Not Wait to Be Discovered!

No matter how great you are, or how great you believe yourself to be, you must take advantage of opportunities to market yourself to prospective schools:

- *Create a student profile on web sites like www.zinch.com that may attract the attention of college admissions officers looking for students from your gender or ethnic group; or from your geographical location; or with your talents and interests.*

- *Accurately and thoughtfully complete the PSAT questionnaire.*

- *Attend programs on campus and get to know professors, coaches, and admissions officers.*

- *Instead of becoming good at a lot of things, become great at something that will attract the attention of a college.*

- *Keep a business card folder and stay in contact with admissions officers.*

- *Never squander the opportunity to make a world class first impression!*

APPENDIX II

COLLEGE PLANNING ACTIVITY

Putting the Pieces Together

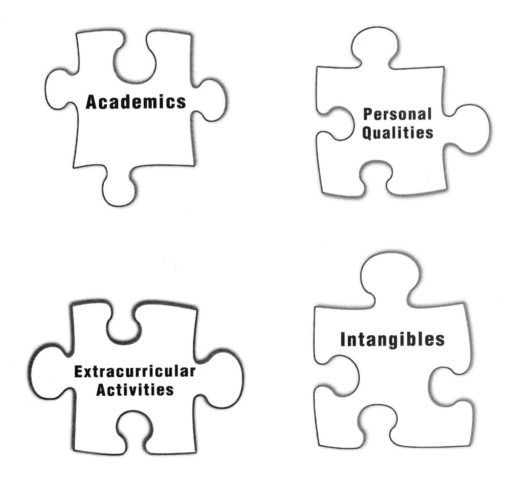

College Planning Illustration

My Dream

A comprehensive college-bound plan will include academics, extracurricular activities, personal qualities, and intangibles that are consistent with your college and career dreams and aspirations. The following illustration reflects the types of things that you must consider within each area.

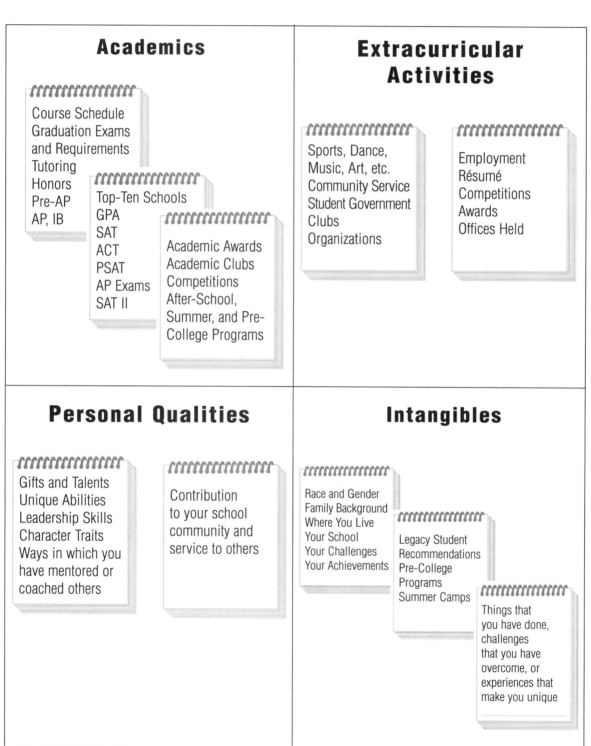

Academics

Course Schedule
Graduation Exams and Requirements
Tutoring
Honors
Pre-AP
AP, IB

Top-Ten Schools
GPA
SAT
ACT
PSAT
AP Exams
SAT II

Academic Awards
Academic Clubs
Competitions
After-School, Summer, and Pre-College Programs

Extracurricular Activities

Sports, Dance, Music, Art, etc.
Community Service
Student Government
Clubs
Organizations

Employment
Résumé
Competitions
Awards
Offices Held

Personal Qualities

Gifts and Talents
Unique Abilities
Leadership Skills
Character Traits
Ways in which you have mentored or coached others

Contribution to your school community and service to others

Intangibles

Race and Gender
Family Background
Where You Live
Your School
Your Challenges
Your Achievements

Legacy Student
Recommendations
Pre-College Programs
Summer Camps

Things that you have done, challenges that you have overcome, or experiences that make you unique

Group Instructions

Students may engage in this activity individually or as a group. If the activity is engaged in as a group, the group must agree on one career aspiration as the focus of their college plan.

Beginning Instructions

1. Select a group leader.

2. Select a group member who will be the group's "researcher." This individual will gather information or ask questions on behalf of the group.

3. Select a group member who will be the group's "writer" (someone with good penmanship) who will take notes and write up the group's ideas.

4. Select a "spokesperson" to facilitate the group presentation.

Working Instructions

1. Discuss the career aspirations of each member of the group and select one member and his or her career aspiration to focus your research efforts.

2. Complete each activity by focusing on this person and his or her career aspiration.

Presentation Instructions

1. Assign each group member an area of your plan to present (i.e., academic schedule, extracurricular activities, personal qualities, and intangibles).

2. Share the career aspirations of each group member and explain how this activity will assist each group member in formulating his or her college plan.

3. Be creative!

What type of plan will you need to pursue your career goal?

Before you can develop a college plan you will need to know who you are, the types of opportunities offered in your current school and community, and the types of colleges, technical schools, or other types of postsecondary programs that will help you to pursue your career aspirations. For some students, college will refer to schools offering 4-year undergraduate programs, for other students, college will refer to 2-year community or junior colleges, and for other students, college will refer to trade or technical schools. Whatever your career dreams and aspirations, you must have a plan!

Creating your college plan is like running a 400-meter race. Each 100 meters will require a strategy. The first 100 meters will be academics, the second 100 meters will be your extracurricular activities, the third 100 meters will be your personal qualities, and the final 100 meters will be your intangibles.

Academics

- Meeting high school graduation requirements
- Course work
- Grades
- SAT, ACT, PSAT, and AP scores
- Academic honors and awards

Extracurricular Activities

- Sports
- Clubs
- Student organizations
- Community service
- Work experience

Personal Qualities

- Unique talents and abilities
- Personal achievements

Intangibles

- Ethnicity, gender, family background, and where you live
- Camps, pre-college programs, or special training
- Challenges, triumphs, and experiences
- Legacy student

Activity 1: Self Assessment (p. 10)

Your dreams, and the colleges that may best help you to pursue those dreams should guide your efforts in planning your high school schedule of classes, extracurricular activities, and involvement in student and community organizations.

1. Write down 5 obstacles that you will have to overcome.
2. Write down 5 academic strengths.
3. Write down 5 academic weaknesses.
4. Write down 5 people who support you.
5. Write down 5 high school goals.
6. Write down 5 life goals.

Activity 2: Why do you want to attend college? (p. 26)

Coming to terms with why you would want to attend college will help you to better understand why your academic focus is important.

Answer the following questions:

1. Do you want to go away to college or stay close to home?
2. Do you want to go to college to play a sport?
3. Do you want to go to college to prepare for a career immediately following undergraduate school?
4. Do you want to go to college to prepare for graduate school, law school, or medical school?
5. Do you want to go to college to join a fraternity or sorority?
6. Do you want to go to college to further develop a talent in music, art, dance, or a certain skill?

Activity 3: What is your top-ten list of colleges and universities? (p. 28-29)

By focusing on whether or not a school will meet your needs rather than its national ranking, your list is likely to include schools in each category: Highly Competitive (schools with admission rates under 25 percent); Competitive (schools with admission rates under 50 percent); Traditional (schools where you meet the basic admissions requirements).

Write down the colleges and universities that would best assist you in pursuing your career goals and future aspirations. If you have access to the Internet, complete the research sheet on page 28 for your top school.

Activity 4: Develop a 4-year academic schedule (p. 49)

Perhaps the most important skill that you can develop as a high school student in preparation for admission into and success in college is the ability to communicate your thoughts and ideas—verbally and in writing. When planning your high school course schedule, you should strongly consider such courses as literature, history, philosophy, and statistics.

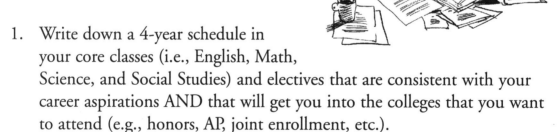

1. Write down a 4-year schedule in your core classes (i.e., English, Math, Science, and Social Studies) and electives that are consistent with your career aspirations AND that will get you into the colleges that you want to attend (e.g., honors, AP, joint enrollment, etc.).

2. Write down your goal for the GPA in the classes that relate directly to your career goal (e.g., art, music, math, science, business, etc.) and your goal for your overall GPA.

3. Write down academic clubs, summer camps, and pre-college programs that can support your academic achievement.

4. Write down when and how many times you will take the PSAT, SAT, and ACT exams.

Activity 5: Develop a 4-year extracurricular activity schedule (p. 62)

Choose extracurricular activities that you will both enjoy and can excel in—activities where you can make a contribution, assume leadership roles, develop your talents, and pursue your passions. Consider activities that will provide opportunities to build relationships with people you enjoy and perhaps lead to scholarship consideration by some of the schools on your top-ten list.

1. Write down any extracurricular activities that you can become involved in AND continue to perform well academically (e.g., sports, band, cheerleading, drama, student government, etc.).

2. Write down any clubs or student organizations that relate to your gifts, talents, or interests.

3. Write down any community or youth programs that you will be involved in throughout your time in high school.

4. Write down any jobs or volunteer programs that you will be involved in.

Activity 6: What are your unique personal qualities?

No matter how you compare to others in terms of grades and test scores, who you are, what you have done, and what you stand for can become the defining factors that convinces an admissions officer that you are a student who would make a noteworthy contribution to his or her college community.

1. Write down all of the positions or offices that you have held or are planning to hold, e.g., captain, president, student council representative. (p. 72)

2. Write down any unique gifts and talents that you have or are developing, e.g., dance, music, band, art, cheerleading, athletics, or leadership. (p. 76)

Final Activity: Write a one-page essay on the topic, "What's your story?" (p. 78)

Your essay provides you with the opportunity to share your story and to celebrate your uniqueness. What are your hopes, your dreams, your struggles, and your triumphs?

As you prepare your essay, consider the following questions. Answering these questions may help you develop a vision of what a college education will do for you, your family, and your community.

1. What makes you special?

2. What obstacles have you overcome?

3. What dreams and aspirations will a college education assist you in pursuing?

4. What people or events have inspired or encouraged you to attend college?

5. How will your college education benefit your family and community?

Final question: Who are the people, i.e., teachers, counselors, mentors, administrators, or coaches who can write a glowing letter of recommendation for you?

APPENDIX III

SAMPLE APPLICATION

On the following pages is a sample application, with supplements. Please note that your application will be reviewed along with hundreds if not thousands of other applications. Your application should be neatly typed, free of typographical errors, and accurate (i.e., your address, social security number, grades, test scores, etc.).

This student completed the Common Application (www.commonapp.org) and the Amherst College supplements for athletics and Fine Arts.

COMMON APPLICATION™
2005–2006

APPLICATION FOR UNDERGRADUATE ADMISSION

The member colleges and universities listed above fully support the use of this form. No distinction will be made between it and the college's own form. Please type or print in black ink.

Be sure to follow the instructions on the cover page of the Common Application booklet to complete, copy, and file your application with any one or several of the member colleges and universities.

OPTIONAL DECLARATION OF EARLY DECISION/EARLY ACTION

Complete this section **ONLY** for the individual college to which you are applying ED or EA. It is your responsibility to follow that college's instructions regarding early admission, including obtaining and submitting any ED/EA form provided by that college. *Do NOT complete this ED/EA section on copies of your application submitted to colleges for Regular Decision or Rolling Admission.*

College Name: AMHERST COLLEGE   Deadline: 11/15/05

[X] Early Decision   [ ] Early Action   [ ] EASC

PERSONAL DATA

Legal Name: SMITH (Last/Family)   KIMBERLY (First)   TIFFANY (Middle (complete))   (Jr., etc.)   F (Gender)
Enter name exactly as it appears on passports or other official documents.

Nickname (choose only one): KIM   Former last name(s) if any _____

Are you applying as a [X] freshman or [ ] transfer student?   For the term beginning FALL - 2006

Birthdate 01/10/1988 (mm/dd/yyyy)   E-mail Address yourname@yourname.com

Permanent Home Address 5144 S. MLKING DRIVE (Number and Street)   Permanent Home Phone (889) 889-8989

CHICAGO (City or Town)   IL (State/Province)   COOK (Country)   60615 - (Zip Code or Postal Code)

If different from above, please give your mailing address for all admission correspondence.

Mailing Address (from ____ (mm/yyyy) to ____ (mm/yyyy)) _____ (Number and Street)

____ (City or Town)   ____ (State/Province)   ____ (Country)   ____ (Zip Code or Postal Code)

Phone at mailing address (____) ____   Cell phone (889) 889-1234

Citizenship [X] US citizen   [ ] Dual US citizen; please specify other country of citizenship _____

[ ] US Permanent Resident visa; citizen of _____   Alien Registration Number _____

[ ] Other Citizenship _____ (Country(ies))   _____ (Visa type)

If you are not a US citizen and live in the United States, how long have you been in the country? _____

Possible area(s) of academic concentration/major(s) FINE ARTS - BLACK STUDIES - PSYCHOLOGY or undecided [ ]

Special college or division if applicable _____

Possible career or professional plans FINE ART, ILLUSTRATION, ANIMATION or undecided [ ]

Will you be a candidate for financial aid? [X] Yes   [ ] No   If yes, the appropriate form(s) was/will be filed on 11/1/05

The following items are *optional*. No information you provide will be used in a discriminatory manner.

Place of birth CHICAGO (City)   IL (State/Province)   COOK (Country)   Social Security Number (if any) 998 30 9999

First language, if other than English _____   Language spoken at home ENGLISH

If you wish to be identified with a particular ethnic group, please check all that apply

[X] African American, Black   [ ] Mexican American, Chicano
[ ] Native American, Alaska Native (tribal affiliation ____ enrolled ____)   [ ] Native Hawaiian, Pacific Islander
[ ] Asian American (countries of family's origin ____)   [ ] Puerto Rican
[ ] Asian, including Indian Subcontinent (countries ____)   [ ] White or Caucasian
[ ] Hispanic, Latino (countries ____)   [ ] Other (specify ____)

2005–2006   **AP-1**

Adelphi · Agnes Scott · Albertson · Albion · Albright · Alfred · Allegheny · American · Amherst · Antioch · Arcadia · Assumption · College of the Atlantic · Austin College · Babson · Baldwin–Wallace · Bard · Barnard · Bates · Beloit · Bennington · Bentley · Binghamton · Birmingham–Southern · Boston College · Boston U. · Bowdoin · Bradley · Brandeis · Bryant · Bryn Mawr · Bucknell · Butler · California Lutheran · Carleton · Carnegie Mellon · Case Western Reserve · Cazenovia · Centenary (La.) · Centre · Chatham · Claremont McKenna · Clark U. · Clarkson U. · Coe · Colby · Colby–Sawyer · Colgate · Colorado College · Concordia College (N.Y.) · Connecticut College · Converse · Cornell College · Cornell U. · U. of Dallas · Dartmouth · Davidson · U. of Delaware · Denison · U. of Denver · DePauw · Dickinson · Dominican U. (Calif.) · Drew · Duke · Earlham · Eckerd · Elizabethtown · Elmira · Embry–Riddle · Emmanuel College (Mass.) · Emory · Eugene Lang · Fairfield · Findlay · Fisk · Florida Southern · Fordham · Franklin & Marshall · Furman · George Fox · George Washington · Gettysburg · Gonzaga · Goucher · Grinnell · Guilford · Gustavus Adolphus · Hamilton · Hampden–Sydney · Hampshire · Hanover · Hartwick · Harvard · Harvey Mudd · Haverford · Hendrix · Hiram · Hobart & William Smith · Hofstra · Hollins · Holy Cross · Hood · Illinois Wesleyan · Iona · Ithaca · John Carroll · Johns Hopkins · Juniata · Kalamazoo · Kenyon · Knox · La Roche · La Salle · La Verne · Lafayette · Lake Forest · Lawrence · Le Moyne · Lehigh · Lesley · Lewis & Clark · Linfield · Loyola College · Loyola U. (La.) · Luther · Macalester · U. of Maine (Farmington) · U. of Maine (Orono) · Manhattan · Manhattanville · Marietta · Marlboro · Marquette · Mary Washington · McDaniel · Merrimack · U. of Miami (Fla.) · Miami U. (Ohio) · Middlebury · Mills · Monmouth · Moravian · Morehouse · Mount St.Vincent · Mt.Holyoke · Muhlenberg · Naropa · Nazareth · New College (Fla.) · New England College · U. of New Hampshire · College of New Jersey · New York U. · Northeastern U. · Northland · Notre Dame (Md.) · Notre Dame de Namur · Oberlin · Occidental · Oglethorpe · Ohio Wesleyan · Pace · U. of the Pacific · Pitzer · Pomona · U. of Portland · Presbyterian · Prescott · Princeton · Providence · Puget Sound · Queens U. (N.C.) · Randolph–Macon · Randolph–Macon Woman's · Redlands · Reed · Regis College · Regis U. · Rensselaer · Rhodes · Rice · U. of Richmond · Rider · Ripon · U. of Rochester · Rochester Inst. of Tech. · Roger Williams · Rollins · St. Anselm · St. Benedict & St. John's · St. Joseph's College (Me.) · St. Joseph's U. · St. Lawrence · St. Leo · St. Louis U. · St. Mary's College (Calif.) · St. Mary's College (Ind.) · St. Michael's · St. Norbert · St. Olaf · St. Peter's · St. Vincent · Salem (N.C.) · Salve Regina · U. of San Diego · U. of San Francisco · Santa Clara · College of Santa Fe · Sarah Lawrence · Scranton · Scripps · Seattle U. · Seton Hill · Sewanee · Simmons · Skidmore · Smith · Southern Maine · Southern Methodist · Southern New Hampshire · Southwestern U. · Spelman · Spring Hill · Stetson · Stevens Inst. of Tech · Stonehill · Suffolk · Susquehanna · Swarthmore · Sweet Briar · Syracuse · U. of Tampa · TCU · Transylvania · Trinity College (Conn.) · Trinity U. · Tufts · Tulane · Tulsa · Union College (N.Y.) · Ursinus · Utica · Valparaiso · Vanderbilt · Vassar · U. of Vermont · Villanova · Wabash · Wagner · Wake Forest · Washington College · Washington U. (Mo.) · Washington & Jefferson · Washington & Lee · Webster · Wellesley · Wells · Wesleyan · Westminster (Mo.) · Westminster (Pa.) · Wheaton (Mass.) · Wheelock · Whitman · Whittier · Widener · Willamette · William & Mary · William Jewell · Williams · Wilson · Wittenberg · Wofford · Wooster · WPI · Xavier (Ohio) · Yale

SCHOOL REPORT

The member colleges and universities listed above fully support the use of this form. No distinction will be made between it and the college's own form. Please type or print in black ink.

TO THE APPLICANT

After filling in the information below, give this form to your guidance counselor.

Birthdate **01/10/1988** Gender **F** Social Security No. **998-30-9999**
mm/dd/yyyy *(Optional)*

Student Name **SMITH** **KIMBERLY** **TIFFANY**
Last/Family *First* *Middle (complete)* *Jr., etc.*

Address **5144 SOUTH MLKING DRIVE** **CHICAGO, IL** **USA** **60615**
Number and Street *City or Town* *State/Province* *Country* *Zip Code or Postal Code*

Current year courses—please indicate title, level (AP, IB, advanced honors, etc.) and credit value of all courses you are taking this year.

First Semester/Trimester	Second Semester/Trimester	Third Trimester
AP ART: 2-D DESIGN 1.0	2-D DESIGN II 1.0	
AP PSYCHOLOGY .5	AP PSYCHOLOGY .5	
AP ENVIRONMENTAL SCIENCE .5	AP ENVIRONMENTAL SCIENCE .5	
JEWELRY DESIGN I .5	AP STATISTICS 1.0	
WORLD LITERATURE .5	POLITICAL SCIENCE .5	
BRITISH LITERATURE .5	US HISTORY B .5	
JEWELRY DESIGN II .5		

Please detach along perforation

TO THE SECONDARY SCHOOL GUIDANCE COUNSELOR

Attach applicant's official transcript, including courses in progress, a school profile, and transcript legend. (Please check transcript copies for readability.) After filling in the blanks below, use both sides of this form to describe the applicant. Please provide all available information for this candidate. *Be sure to sign below.*

Class rank _____ in a class of _____ , covering a period from _____ to _____
(mm/yyyy) *(mm/yyyy)*

The rank is ☐ weighted ☐ unweighted. How many students share this rank? _____

If a precise rank is not available, please indicate rank to the nearest tenth from the top _____

Cumulative GPA _____ on a _____ scale, covering a period from _____ to _____
(mm/yyyy) *(mm/yyyy)*

This GPA is ☐ weighted ☐ unweighted. The school's passing mark is _____

Percentage of graduating class attending: _____ four-year _____ two-year institutions

S.S. graduation date _____

Are classes taken on a block schedule?
☐ yes ☐ no

If yes, in what year did block scheduling begin?

Highest grade/GPA in class _____

In comparison with other college preparatory students *at our school*, the applicant's course selection is
☐ most demanding ☐ very demanding ☐ demanding ☐ average ☐ less than demanding

Counselor's Name Mr./Mrs./Ms _____
Please print or type

Signature _____ **Date** _____

Position _____

School _____

Counselor's Address _____

Counselor's Phone (_____) _____ Counselor's Fax (_____) _____
Area Code *Number* *Ext.* *Area Code* *Number*

Secondary School CEEB/ACT Code _____ Counselor's E-mail _____

EDUCATIONAL DATA

Secondary school you now attend (or from which you graduated) _____ Date of entry 08/02

Address D U S A B L E H I G H S C H O O L   CEEB/ACT code 9 9 9 4 6 9 1
Number and Street

4900 S. WABASH AVENUE   CHICAGO, IL   USA   60615
City or Town   *State/Province*   *Country*   *Zip Code or Postal Code*

Date of secondary graduation 05/06   Type of school [X] public [ ] private [ ] parochial [ ] home school

Guidance Counselor's Name Mr./Mrs./Ms MS. CHERYL M. GHOLAR   Position COUNSELOR

Counselor's E-mail _____ Phone (889) 999-9999 x173 Fax (889) 999-8888
mycounselor@cps.k12.ga.us   *Area Code*   *Number*   *Ext.*   *Area Code*   *Number*

List all other secondary schools, including summer schools and programs you have attended beginning with ninth grade.

Name of School	Location (City, State/Province, Zip, Country)	Dates Attended
CHICAGO PUBLIC SCHOOLS	ONLINE PROGRAM	6/04-7/04
ILLINOIS VIRTUAL SCHOOL		6/05-7/05

List all colleges/universities at which you have taken courses for credit; list names of courses taken and grades earned on a separate sheet.
Please have an official transcript sent from each institution as soon as possible.

Name of College/University & CEEB/ACT Code	Location (City, State/Province, Zip, Country)	Degree Candidate?	Dates Attended
		[ ]	
		[ ]	
		[ ]	

[ ] Not currently attending school   [ ] Graduated from secondary school early.
Describe in detail, here or on a separate sheet, your activities since last enrolled.

TEST INFORMATION

Be sure to note the tests required for each institution to which you are applying. The official scores from the appropriate testing agency must be submitted to each institution as soon as possible. Please list your test plans below.

ACT	Date taken/ to be taken	English	Math	Science	Composite	Combination English/Writing
	06/04	30	28	30	29	
	Date taken/ to be taken	English	Math	Science	Composite	Combination English/Writing
	Date taken/ to be taken	English	Math	Science	Composite	Combination English/Writing

SAT I or SAT Reasoning Tests	Date taken/ to be taken	Verbal/Critical Reading	Math	Writing	Date taken/ to be taken	Verbal/Critical Reading	Math	Writing	Date taken/ to be taken	Verbal/Critical Reading	Math	Writing

SAT II or Subject Tests	Date taken/ to be taken	Subject	Score	Date taken/ to be taken	Subject	Score	Date taken/ to be taken	Subject	Score
	Date taken/ to be taken	Subject	Score	Date taken/ to be taken	Subject	Score	Date taken/ to be taken	Subject	Score

Test of English as a second language (TOEFL or other exam)	Test	Date taken/ to be taken	Score	Test	Date taken/ to be taken	Score

OPTIONAL ATHLETIC
BACKGROUND SUPPLEMENT

PLEASE MAIL TO:
Office of Admission
Amherst College
PO Box 5000
Amherst, MA 01002–5000

PERSONAL DATA

Check One ☒ Early Decision ☐ Regular Decision

Legal name WYNN   KIMBERLY   TIFFANY   Gender ☐ Male ☒ Female
last/family   first   middle (complete)   jr., etc.

Mailing address (use from   Permanent   )
                            date   to   date

5 1 4 4   S O U T H   M L K I N G   D R I V E
number and street

C H I C A G O   I L   U S A   6 0 6 1 5
city or town   state   country   zip code + 4 or postal code

Phone at mailing address 7 7 0   5 8 7 - 4 3 9 5 Permanent home phone S A M E
                         area code   number   area code   number

E-mail address y o u r n a m e @ y o u r n a m e . c o m

Secondary School DU SABLE HIGH SCHOOL School address 4900 S. WABASH AVE
                                                     number and street

C H I C A G O   I L   U S A   6 0 6 1 5
city or town   state   country   zip code + 4 or postal code

The following item is optional: Social Security number, if any   9 9 8 - 3 0 - 9 9 9 9

INSTRUCTIONS

If you anticipate participating in varsity athletics at Amherst College, please complete the grid below. List any team sports played in order of their importance to you.

SPORT	YEARS PLAYED 9	10	11	12	LETTERS JV	VARSITY	EVENT OR POSITION	COACH	VARSITY CAPTAIN
LACROSSE			X	X		2	MIDFIELD	HAL	
SOFTBALL	X	X	X		1	2	1B, SS, CF	WOODALL	
TRACK	X	X				2	100, 200, 400	PARKS	CO-CAPTAIN

Please list any times, records, awards, etc. _____

_____

_____

Optional: Height _____   Weight _____

OPTIONAL ARTS BACKGROUND SUPPLEMENT

PERSONAL DATA

Check One ☒ Early Decision ☐ Regular Decision

Legal name SMITH   KIMBERLY   TIFFANY   Gender ☐ Male ☒ Female
last/family   first   middle (complete)   jr., etc.

Mailing address (use from Permanent)
                         date   to   date

5144 S. MLKING DRIVE
number and street

CHICAGO   IL   USA   60615-0010
city or town   state   country   zip code + 4 or postal code

Phone at mailing address 889 889-8989 Permanent home phone SAME
                         area code   number   area code   number

E-mail address yourname@yourname.com

The following item is optional: Social Security number, if any 998-30-9999

PLEASE CHECK MEDIUM

☐ **MUSIC**

Instrument _____ Voice (part) _____

Composition _____ World Music Tradition _____

Song Writing _____ Other _____

☐ **THEATER AND DANCE**

☒ **VISUAL ARTS**

If you've made a substantial commitment of time and energy to one or more of the arts and you wish to have that considered as part of your application, please

1. complete this form
2. have an instructor who is familiar with your work send us a letter of recommendation.

Music

3. attach a résumé to this form that summarizes your experience with instrument, voice, and/or composition, giving years studied, name(s) of teacher(s) or group(s), repertoire or awards.

4. attach an audiotape or CD, no longer than 10 minutes, to this form that shows contrasting examples of expression and technique. **Please include a list below of what is on the tape or CD.** Do not submit audiotapes of chorus, ensembles or other groups. **Please do not submit videotapes.**

Theater and Dance

3. attach a résumé to this form.
4. attach an additional copy of your Supplemental Essay (from the Supplement to the Common Application).
   Please do not submit videotapes.

Visual Arts

3. attach a résumé to this form that gives dates, institution, and a brief description for each course or workshop. Describe other related experience.
4. attach one sheet of slides of your work, including at least three drawings. **Please do not submit originals of your work or videotapes.**

No materials will be forwarded to an arts department until all four components of your portfolio arrive.

All materials must be received at least two weeks before the application deadline. Please send copies only; we are unable to return supplementary materials.

Index

4 x 4 Block Schedule, 49, 52

A High School Plan, i, iii-iv, vii, 1, 41-44, 80, 85, 87, 90, 92, 120
A Middle School Plan, iv, viii, 120
Academic
 Bowl, 62
 Camps, 55
 Clubs, 44
 Data, 108
 Honors, vi, 45
 Success, viii, 43
 Support, vi, 42, 45
Accelerated Math, 49
ACT, 92
ACT Code, 22, 106
ACT Prep Programs, 23
Advanced Placement, 36, 98
Advanced Topics in Physics, 49
Algebra, 30, 39, 49, 52, 91, 99
Allen, Andrew, 34
American College Testing Exam, 56
Amherst College, v, vii, 49, 60, 111-112
AP
 ART, 49, 113
 Art Portfolio, 49
 Classes, 1, 36-37, 51, 54, 106
 Calculus AB, 49
 Computer Science, 49, 52
 Environmental Science, 49, 113
 European History, 49
 Exams, 59, 95
 Grade Reports, 36
 Language, 49
 Literature, 49
 Music Theory, 49
 Physics B, 49
 Program, 92
 Psychology, 49, 113
 Scholar, 36-37
 Scores, 104
 Spanish Language, 49
 Statistics, 113
 U. S. History, 49
 World History, 49
Application
 Deadlines, 28, 93, 103
 Fee, 103-104
 Package, vi-vii, 91, 104
 Package Checklist, 104
 Packages, 22-23, 93-94
Arts Magnet Seal, 31
Athletic Conference, 98
Athletic Data, 108
Athletic Profile, 108

Be The Captain of Your Ship, iv
Biology, 49, 62, 82
Block Schedule, 52

Bowie State University, 60
Bridgewater College, 60
Brown, 98
Calculus, 49, 99
Camps, 16, 22-23, 34, 55, 71
Campus Visits, 27
Career Goal, 108
CEEB, 22, 106
Chemistry, 39, 49
Chowan College, 60
City College of
 San Francisco, 60
 New York, 60
Class Rank, 8, 40, 47, 54, 106, 108
Clemson University, 60
College Admissions Trade Secrets, 34
College
 Affiliations, 26
 Application Organizer, 103
 Board, 33, 98
 English, 49
 Fairs, 23, 27-28, 48
 Information, 22, 29, 56, 88
 Literacy Quiz, 1-2, 7, 98
 Literacy Quiz Answer Key, 98
 Preparatory Diploma, 31
 Tour Checklist, 28
 Tours, 27
College-Bound Athletes, 30
Columbia, 61, 98
Common Application, 89, 91-92, 111
Competitive Schools, 29, 79, 81
Cooper Union, 60
Core Course GPA, 108
Cornell, 98
Course Work, vi, 34, 53
Critical Reading, 3, 57-59, 98-99
Critical Reading Section, 57-58
CSS Profile, 91-93

Dartmouth, vii, 98
Diversity, 28
DRN, 24, 95
Duke University, 60

Early Action, 93
Early Decision, v, vii, 6, 94, 101
East Carolina University, 60
EFC, 6, 94, 100
Electives, 30, 49, 54
End-of-Grade, 30
EOCT, 32
EOG, 32
Essay, 57-58, 80, 83-84, 87, 89-90
Estimated Probability of Competing in Athletics Beyond High School, 70
Exit Exams, vi, 30, 32-33, 93
Expected Family Contribution, 94, 100

FAFSA, 6, 24, 89, 91-95, 100, 106, 108
Fairmont State College, 60
Federal Student Aid, 100
Fee Waiver, 91, 104
Financial
 Aid, vi, 1, 23, 28, 83, 89, 92-93, 95, 100, 103
 Checklist, 88
 Information, 22
Fine Arts, 49, 51, 111-112
Florida State University, 60
Follow Your Dreams, iv, 10, 120
Foreign Language, 7, 30, 49, 51, 54, 62, 82
Forensics, 49
Foundation for Ensuring Access and Equity, 92
Freshman Language Arts, 49
From High School to the Future: Potholes on the Road to College, 81
Frostburg University, 60

Geometry, 49, 99
George Mason University, 60
Georgetown University, 60
Gifted Internship, 49
Goddard, John, 19
Grade Point Average, 31-32, 39-40, 99
Guitar, 49

Hampton University, 60
Harvard, 60, 98
HBCU, 3, 98
High School
 Course Offerings, 47
 Graduation Requirements, 1, 30, 49
 Schedule, 10, 36, 49
 Worksheets, vi
Highly Selective, 60-61
Historically Black Colleges, 98
Honors
 Accelerated Math, 49
 Algebra II, 39, 49, 52
 American Lit, 49
 Biology, 49
 Bio Chemistry, 49
 Chemistry, 49
 Classes, 35, 39, 51, 54
 Economics, 49
 Freshman Language Arts, 49
 Junior American Lit/Comp, 49
 Physics, 49
 Pre-Calculus, 49, 52
 Sophomore Language Arts, 49
 Spanish Culture, 49
 Spanish
  II, 49
  III, 49
  IV, 49, 52

www.rspublishing • (800) 524-2813 • (770) 518-0369 • FAX (770) 587-0862
Payment May Be Made By Money Order • Check • Credit Card • Purchase Order

Item #	Description	Unit Price	X Quantity	= Total
5003	Follow Your Dreams: *Lessons That I Learned in Schl*	7.95		
6545	College Planning Notebook (binder & H.S. inserts)	19.95		
6555	College Planning Notebook (3-ring binder only)	5.95		
6903	A High School Plan...College-Bound Dreams	19.95		
6905	A High School Plan...*Student Workbook*	15.95		
6602	College Planning for High School Students	5.95		
6901	A Middle School Plan...College-Bound Dreams	15.95		
6906	A Middle School Plan...*Student Workbook*	15.95		
6601	College Planning for Middle School Students	5.95		
7201	Ten Steps to Helping Your Child Succeed in School	9.95		
7202	Ten Steps to Helping Your Child...*Workbook*	15.95		
6500	College-Bound Backpack	7.95		
5601	The Eagles who Thought They were Chickens: Book	4.95		
5603	Eagles: *Student Activity Book*	5.95		
5602	Eagles: *Teacher's Guide*	9.95		
6510	College-Bound Pen-Highlighter	1.95		
6530	College-Bound Student Planner	7.95		

Charge my:　❑ Visa　❑ Mastercard　❑ Discover　❑ American Express

_____

Account Number   Security Code

_____

Expiration Date   Signature

SUBTOTAL $ _____

Shipping (Subtotal x 10%)   _____

Add Handling   3.50

Georgia residents
add 6% Sales Tax   _____

DATE: _____   TOTAL _____

RISING SUN PUBLISHING
P.O. Box 70906
Marietta, GA 30007-0906

RISING SUN
PUBLISHING

☎ Phone toll-free: **1.800.524.2813**
FAX: **1.770.587.0862**
e-mail: orderdesk@rspublishing.com
web site: http://www.rspublishing.com

Name _____

Address _____

_____

City_____ State_____ Zip _____

Day Phone (_____) _____ E-mail : _____

❑ *Check if you would like to receive our free monthly E-mail newsletter*